NANCY HANKS LINCOLN

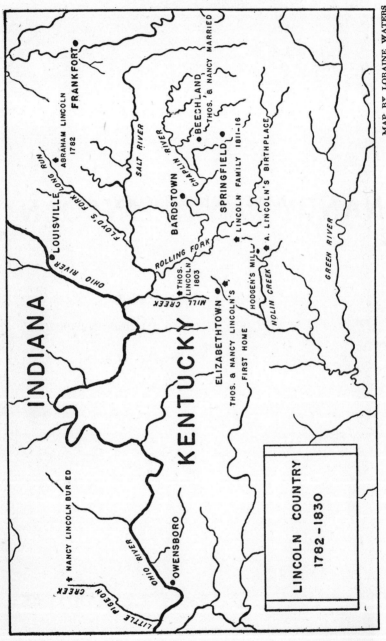

INDIANA

KENTUCKY

OHIO RIVER

LITTLE PIGEON CREEK
+ NANCY LINCOLN BUR ED
• OWENSBORO

FRANKFORT •
ABRAHAM LINCOLN
1782
• LOUISVILLE
LONG RUN
FLOYD'S FORK
SALT RIVER
BARDSTOWN •
CHAPLIN RIVER
ROLLING FORK
MILL CREEK
• THOS. LINCOLN 1803
ELIZABETHTOWN •
THOS. & NANCY LINCOLN'S
FIRST HOME
• BEECH LAND
THOS. & NANCY MARRIED
• SPRINGFIELD
LINCOLN FAMILY 1811-16
• A. LINCOLN'S BIRTHPLACE
• HODGEN'S MILL
NOLIN CREEK
GREEN RIVER

LINCOLN COUNTRY
1782-1830

MAP BY LORAINE WATERS

NANCY HANKS LINCOLN

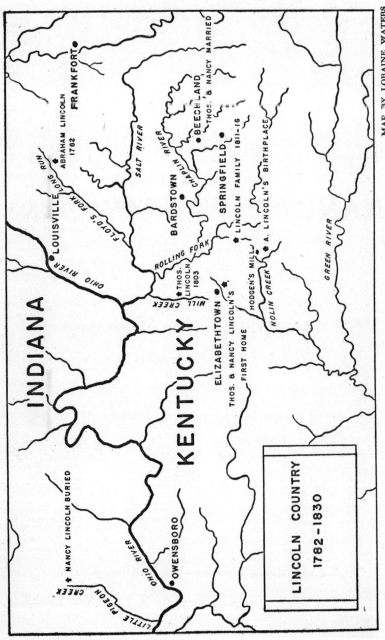

MAP BY LORAINE WATERS

INDIANA

KENTUCKY

NANCY LINCOLN BURIED

LITTLE PIGEON CREEK

OHIO RIVER

OWENSBORO

FRANKFORT

ABRAHAM LINCOLN
1782

LOUISVILLE

LONG RUN

FLOYD'S FORK

OHIO RIVER

SALT RIVER

CHAPLIN RIVER

BARDSTOWN

BEECH LAND
THOS. & NANCY MARRIED

SPRINGFIELD

LINCOLN FAMILY 1811-16

A. LINCOLN'S BIRTHPLACE

ROLLING FORK

MILL CREEK

THOS. LINCOLN'S
1803

ELIZABETHTOWN

THOS. & NANCY LINCOLN'S
FIRST HOME

HODGEN'S MILL

NOLIN CREEK

GREEN RIVER

LINCOLN COUNTRY
1782-1830

NANCY HANKS LINCOLN

A FRONTIER PORTRAIT

by Harold E. Briggs, Ph.D.

PROFESSOR OF HISTORY, SOUTHERN ILLINOIS UNIVERSITY

and Ernestine B. Briggs, M.A.

1952 : BOOKMAN ASSOCIATES : NEW YORK

973.7092
B76N

35565
October, 1957

In Memory
of
Sarah Yeager Bennett
Who knew the ways of a later frontier

"In life and death her brief story was that of the American pioneer woman."

Dictionary of American Biography, Volume XI, page 243, (Edited by Dumas Malone, New York, 1933)

Contents

Preface

Who was Nancy Hanks Lincoln? What kind of woman was she? There is in existence, so far as is known, no picture of her, nor any complete description. Any literary portrait of her must therefore be developed slowly, and with great patience. One cannot paint it with swift phrases. Rather, it is as if we wove first one thread and then another, many of them sombre, few of any apparent importance or value, until gradually the story of a frontier girl called Nancy Hanks begins to take shape.

The background before which the figure of this girl stands is of great importance in interpreting that story. She was a product of three frontiers: Virginia, Kentucky, and Indiana. Much that will be noted in Nancy Lincoln is already familiar to us in another figure—that of her famous son, Abraham Lincoln.

The incidents recorded on the following pages are not imaginary, but are in existence in history and literature. The purpose of this volume is to bring together the widely scattered materials dealing with the subject, and, as far as possible, to separate tradition from fact. If an element of the legendary still seems to linger, it is not because the authors have not made every possible effort to present a true and accurate picture of the life of this pioneer woman as she moved westward with the ever shifting frontier of settlement, but because so important a person long ago became a vital part of the great Lincoln story: half-myth, half-fact.

Harold E. Briggs
Ernestine Bennett Briggs

Carbondale, Illinois
September 12, 1952

Bibliographical Note

There is, undoubtedly, no American about whom more has been written than Abraham Lincoln. In much of this material, his mother, Nancy Hanks Lincoln, is at least briefly mentioned. There has also been a growing body of materials dealing with the various frontiers on which Nancy Hanks and Thomas Lincoln were born and lived.

The authors have read widely in all types of source materials. They have traveled in the Lincoln country in Kentucky and Indiana, and availed themselves of various court records to which their attention had been directed by the early research of Miss Ida Tarbell, and the later efforts of Dr. Louis A. Warren and the Lincoln National Life Insurance Company. To the latter two—through the files of *Lincoln Lore*—a debt of gratitude is expressly owed, especially for material relating to the Lincolns and Hankses before they came to Kentucky.

This has been a work of many years. Innumerable books and articles have been read; documents studied; the accuracy of statements thoughtfully gauged; and it is hoped the authors have accomplished a purpose first attempted a decade ago: to present as real (and truthful) a picture as possible of the mother of one of the greatest Presidents of the United States of America. Photography was unknown while she lived; apparently no wandering artist or silhouette cutter ever left a record of this frontier girl; and by the time—through her son's fame—she became important, many years had elasped.

It has not been an easy task. Through the years legend has obscured fact; paragraph after paragraph has been rewritten because of a new statement, or a more recently discovered record. Acknowledgement is here made to all the writers who have written in the field of the frontier and that of Lincolniana.

I
The
Wilderness
Trail

It was the year 1782. Half of Virginia seemed to be pouring west along the Wilderness Trail. All through the eighties they were to come—the men on foot with their guns ready for use, driving their stock before them, leading pack horses which carried the little wealth they could bring from their eastern homes. There were women, some walking, others riding, many with children in their laps, and often with other children swung in baskets on horses. The Wilderness Road was well named, for this was still virgin territory, where wagons could not penetrate. At night, when camp was made, the women drew within the welcome light of the fire, for Indians might very well be within a stone's throw, and it was possible that before dawn there might be heard the war cry of the red men. But still the pioneers came, for they had heard tales of a land of great fertility, a land where corn would grow easily, and where great estates could be carved from miles of rich soil. It was not hunting, nor the wild life of the migrant, that called most of these pioneers, but the fertile acres of Kentucky.

There were many reasons why Virginians and Carolinians looked westward in those days, and took the trails into the wilderness. During and after the American Revolution, Tories were sometimes mistreated, and in many cases their homes and lands were taken from them, and they were driven from the communities in which they had lived. For many of these, their only refuge was the frontier. The Revolutionary soldiers of Virginia were unpaid, and the state used its western lands to settle its debts. Also, the rate of taxation in Virginia was high, and the average man found it difficult to pay his taxes and still have enough to live on. There were men like Daniel Boone, who was very poor, and hoped to acquire a fortune in the west. The decreasing fertility of Virginia's soil was an added factor. Which of these reasons, or what combination, brought the Lincolns and the Hankses, who came in that emigration of the eighties, across the mountains into Kentucky, is not known. Perhaps they were only following a pattern set by several generations: following the frontier as it pushed ever westward.

This Wilderness Road they traveled had once been a succession of irregular woodland paths trodden down and worn bare by buffalo, and by Indian hunters and Indian war parties. For Kentucky was a hunting ground for the red men from the south, and especially for those from across the Ohio. White men had wandered into it from the east, and had brought back tales of its beauty and promises of wealth, so that by 1770 the settlers of Virginia and North Carolina knew vaguely of this great territory beyond the mountains. The most romantic spot along the Wilderness Trail was Cumberland Gap. Located where the states of Virginia, Kentucky, and Tennessee meet, it was the scene of innumerable conflicts between Indians and white men, and was the point where settlers poured into the new west. It had been discovered in 1674 by an illiterate frontiersman, Gabriel Arthur, contrary to the old couplet:

> The first white man in Cumberland Gap
> Was Doctor Walker, an English chap.

Walker rediscovered and named this gap in 1750. Through Cumberland Gap ran the Great Warrior Path, along which the Shawnees and Iroquois traveled on their way to attack the southern tribes. One may stand today, said Frederick Jackson Turner, at Cumberland Gap and watch—in retrospect—all of American civilization pass in single file—the buffalo, going down to the salt springs, "the Indian, the fur-trader . . . (the) hunter, . . . the pioneer farmer."

Arthur, Walker, Christopher Gist, and nameless hunters and traders who traveled the Wilderness Trail and penetrated into the area which became Kentucky, aroused an increasing interest in this new west. At the time of the Revolution—at the time, back in Virginia, a child named Thomas Lincoln, born in 1776, was growing to boyhood—no Indian tribe occupied Kentucky. It was, indeed, a sort of no-man's land. Teeming with game, it attracted hunters, but the powerful Iroquois prevented any tribe settling here. Already, in the conflict between the red men, it had won the name of a "dark and bloody ground."

It was, in the end, Daniel Boone who became most closely associated with it. He had learned about it from John Finley, a trapper and adventurer, with whom he had become acquainted when he had gone from North Carolina to participate in Braddock's fatal march across the Pennsylvania mountains to Fort Duquesne. As early as 1767, Boone, remembering those glowing tales of a hunter's paradise, had attempted to reach Kentucky, but had failed because. he had started too late, and winter had come early, with deep snows.

Then Finley had turned up in the settlement in the valley of the Yadkin where the Boones were living, and in May, 1769, Daniel Boone, Finley, and four other men started west, passing through Cumberland Gap into Kentucky. Boone spent two years there, exploring and hunting, having many of those experiences now associated with his name, and becoming so enamored of the country that he made up his mind to return with his family to live there. This plan was not realized for some time, but he continued to make trips into Kentucky, becoming more enthusiastic over the possibilities of the territory each time, and communicating that enthusiasm to other prospective settlers, among them, no doubt, the Lincolns, who were his friends.

In the year 1775 a group of men, led by Richard Henderson, organized the Transylvania Company, whose purpose was to found a western colony. In March of that year, defying the Proclamation of 1763, and also the prohibitions of the colonial governments against unauthorized western settlements, this company concluded an illegal transaction with the Cherokee Indians, whereby the red men ceded to it some twenty million acres of land lying between the Cumberland and Kentucky Rivers, and including a great deal of what are now Kentucky and central Tennessee. Daniel Boone was asked to take a party of men and cut a road to Kentucky, by which the company might enter into possession of its western kingdom. The part of the famous trail which he helped blaze was known as Boone's Trace.

The story of the marking of the Wilderness Road is in itself a tale of adventure. Parts of it had been cleared long before by buffalo and Indian, but other stretches, for miles, had to be cut, and the red men proved most unfriendly. Boone took thirty men for the project, beginning his trace at the Indian treaty ground at Fort Watagua, in what is now eastern Tennessee, going by way of Cumberland Gap and through the rugged mountains and rolling canelands of Kentucky to the mouth of Otter Creek. On the Kentucky

River a site was chosen for a fortified town, and named Boonesborough. Later the road forked at Hazel Patch in Laurel County, one branch leading to Crab Orchard and Danville, and then to the Falls of the Ohio where Louisville developed.

Almost immediately a stream of pioneers in search of western land began pouring over this trail. It was fed by the Great Valley Road which other settlers followed down the Shenandoah and Holston Valleys to Cumberland Gap. Hundreds of pioneers on their way to Kentucky were scalped by Indians, and the Wilderness Road was indeed a dangerous one. For two decades it was little more than a foot path or a pack horse trail, but in 1792 it was widened, by the effort of Kentucky's first governor, Isaac Shelby, to accommodate wagons. In spite of legislation, however, it remained primarily a pack road until Kentucky was well established in the union. Yet each year thousands of settlers entered the state by the Wilderness Trail, and many head of stock were driven east to Virginia and Carolina over this famous road.

2

Abraham

Lincoln

Pioneer

One of the immigrants who traveled the Wilderness Trail in 1782 was Abraham Lincoln, the grandfather of President Lincoln. He had first visited Kentucky when he was thirty-six years old, at which time he was already a prominent man in the Shenandoah Valley. At twenty-six he had been a captain in the Virginia Militia. During the American Revolution he had served as judge advocate in the military courts of Augusta and Rockingham Counties. Abraham was one of five brothers, sons of a prosperous farmer in the Shenandoah Valley named John Lincoln. Only one of these remained in Virginia, the other four migrating west, one to Tennessee, one to Ohio, and the other two—Thomas and Abraham—to Kentucky.

Abraham Lincoln traced his ancestry back to one Samuel Lincoln, who had come from western England to Hingham, Massachusetts, about 1637. This surname was often mispronounced and misspelled, and is found in colonial records as Linken, Linkern, Linkon, Linkhorn, Lingcum, etc., but such spellings are invariably the work of clerks or other official copyists. The eldest son of Lincoln, the pioneer, asserted under oath that his father spelled his name correctly. In fact, down through a period when there were many illiterate men in America, no Lincoln misspelled his name.

Samuel Lincoln's wife was Mary Lyford. Their fourth son, Mordecai, born in 1657, married Sarah Jones, and it is said that the name, Abraham, that of her father, was then introduced into the Lincoln family, where it became a favorite one. The Pilgrims, when they came to America, often called their settlements after their old homes in England, but almost invariably their children born in the New World were given Biblical names. Each generation of Lincolns had its Abraham, its Mordecai, its Isaac, Jacob, Hannah, Mary.

The oldest son of Mordecai and Sarah Lincoln was also named Mordecai. His first wife was Hanah Saltar, and their eldest son was named John. By this time the Lincolns had reached Berks County in Pennsylvania in their westward migration, and there were many settlers by the name of Boone in this area. There were at least five marriages between the Boones and the Lincolns in Pennsylvania. It was at this particular point in their family history that the long friendship between the Boones and the Lincolns began. When this Mordecai Lincoln made his will in 1735, a Boone was named as a trustee to assist his second wife, Mary Robeson Lincoln, in settling the estate, and Squire Boone, the father of Daniel, was one of the appraisers when Mordecai died in 1736. The tradition which came down to President Lincoln—that the Lincolns had once been Quakers, but later "fell away" from that faith—no doubt had its roots in this sojourn in Pennsylvania. The Lincolns probably married into Quaker families.

John Lincoln, who was born in 1716, married Rebecca (Flowers) Morris. Their oldest son, Abraham, the grandfather of the President, was born in Pennsylvania in 1744. They had, in all, nine children, born between 1744 and 1767, and John Lincoln lived to be an old man, for the date of his death is recorded as 1788. Because he left Pennsylvania for Virginia, he was sometimes referred to as "Virginia John." The many descendants of Samuel Lincoln, who had left a large family, included some prominent citizens. Several saw service in the War of the Revolution; others held importan public offices; two were governors of states (one of Maine one of Massachusetts).

It is p obable that Abraham Lincoln made the move to Kentuck under the influence of Daniel Boone. The decision to igrate west was evidently made sometime during the wint r of 1779-1780; for on September 6, 1779, he had bought s me land to increase his Shenandoah Valley farm on Linvi le Creek, but on February 18, 1780, he sold his estate fo "5000 pounds current money of Virginia." Three weeks la ter, he bought his first land warrant in Kentucky - 00 acres, for which he paid 160 pounds. On May 29 he en tered a survey on Long Run at Hughes Station. He had robably helped build Hughes Station, which was erected oy Morgan Hughes in 1780, and stood on Long Run in Jefferson County. It was a weak fort, poorly built, consistin g of eight cabins and four block-houses at the corners. The Lincolns settled on the land on Long Run, probably livi g in one of the cabins in Hughes Station. It was a period when Kentucky settlers found the Indians so troublesome that most emigrants lived in, or close to, forts. In 1784, w en John Filson published his *Discovery, Settlement, and Pr sent State of Kentucke,* there were some 30,000 settlers i the territory, yet there were only 18 houses outside the 52 stations.

Back in Virginia, Abraham Lincoln had married. The date of th s marriage is given as June 1770, and while the name of t e bride is not recorded, it is assumed to have been Bers eba (Herring?), as this is the name of the wife who sign d the deed when he sold his Virginia farm in 1780, and also that of the widow whom he left in Kentucky when he die in 1786. There is a tradition, however, that this was his econd wife, and that his first wife's name was Mary (Shepley?). There were five children: Mordecai, Josiah,

Thomas, Mary, and Nancy, (sometimes given as Nancy Ann, or Ann). In 1782, when the Lincolns started west, Thomas, later the father of President Lincoln, and whose birth date is given as 1776, was still a young child.

The Lincolns joined other emigrants on the Wilderness Road, keeping a sharp outlook for Indians, for, while papers had been signed giving the western lands to white men, the savages did not always seem to understand what this meant, or, perhaps, they understood too well. Abraham must have been acutely aware of the possible dangers, since it is said he had made an earlier trip to Kentucky, and that on his return to Virginia, had been captured by Indians near Danville, made to run the gauntlet, and then released. But the Lincolns reached their destination safely. Abraham had taken with him enough money to enter a considerable tract of land, one which would have made his family wealthy if he had lived long enough to insure its retention. On September 26, 1782, he acquired another land warrant, calling for more than 2000 acres of land, at a price of 3630 pounds. Apparently he made plans to have this grant surveyed, but it was in litigation at the time of his death, and his eldest son, Mordecai, was unable to secure a title to it.

Kentucky had become the country of romance and fable for many Virginians. In 1780–1782 many families had come west. Early in 1780 some three hundred "large family boats" had arrived at the Falls of the Ohio, where Captain Bullitt had surveyed the land seven years before, and in May the legislature of Virginia passed a law for the incorporation of Louisville, which then contained some 600 inhabitants. Abraham Lincoln settled not far from Louisville. Enough settlers had arrived in this area to give some semblance of a social order.

This was frontier country, still, and was to remain so for

a long time, in spite of the large numbers of pioneers pouring in. Most of these were lured west by the promise of land—ever enticing to the Anglo-Saxon. These Virginians were land lovers. There was also the usual froth of idlers and shiftless wanderers and adventurers. Society was the same here as on other frontiers. Human life was almost worthless, for it was of little value in that hard struggle for existence. While life was held in comparative disregard, there was great emphasis on property, and theft was visited not only with punishment, but with severe social proscription. Homicide was punished less severely and less quickly than was horse stealing.

These early Kentuckians were a simple-living and a conscientious people. They meted out a primitive discipline. Sometimes they used the "Law of Moses," or forty lashes, and to petty criminals they applied the "United States flag," or thirteen stripes. Perhaps to them sloth was the worst crime—at least it was the greatest weakness of which a man could be accused. A "Lazy Lawrence" was welcome nowhere. Another fatal weakness was cowardice. Weapons, precious because of their scarcity, were kept for really serious warfare, such as that with Indians or animals, and, when honor must be defended, fists, teeth, and gouging thumbs were used, often with fatal effects.

It was in this frontier society that Thomas Lincoln and Nancy Hanks, both brought west as small children over the Wilderness Trail, grew to maturity. Historians have sometimes termed them illiterate, unambitious, poor, but they were only the products of their era, and no less literate, no less ambitious, no less wealthy, than thousands of their contemporaries. It was not a lavish time, nor were libraries or schools, or any of the other cultural evidences of civilization, to be found in many places in that great wilderness known as Kentucky. They were children of the frontier, and their children were also to be products of a later frontier, for, while America's advancing line of settlement ran ever swiftly westward, it took more than one generation—or five, or ten—to make a nation. The children of Abraham and Bersheba Lincoln might have become influential and wealthy—they had as good lineage and better than many who did—but the force of circumstance decreed otherwise.

If there were not luxury and wealth, there were characteristics in this pioneer society which were to make America great and strong. It took endurance and strength and faith to measure up to the demands of the frontier. It made men like Thomas Lincoln and women like Nancy Hanks and, in time, a man like Abraham Lincoln, in whom the blood of generations of pioneers flowed.

On this Kentucky frontier, there was little outlawry in the early years. One of the most remarkable things about these emigrants from Virginia was their regard for law and their almost infallible instinct for the preservation of their Anglo-Saxon inheritance of legal organization. In all the circumstances of their daily existence, during this period, they may be said to have approached barbarism, yet they were advanced politically. They were children of a race trained for generations in government, and, wherever they went, they formed the town, the county, and the court. The red men, invisible but nevertheless always threatening, always surrounding their feeble settlements, were no detriment to the organization of this new territory according to the ways in which these settlers had been trained in older communities, and, before that, far beyond the ocean.

It is these old court records that are proof of the few facts about the life of Nancy Hanks and of Thomas Lincoln.

Settlers found life here simpler than it had become in the Shenandoah Valley. They dressed in the plainest fashion, in the skins of wild beasts killed by themselves, or in linen stuffs woven by the women. Iron, except in firearms and knives, was almost unknown. For food they depended on game, fish, and roughly ground corn-meal. Money was neither given nor asked, generally, in deals—exchanges were often made by barter, and many children grew up without seeing money. Discomfort was an inmate of most homes. Log cabins were seldom warm or comfortable. For their mode of life many settlers paid heavily, for they suffered from malaria and rheumatic fever, and few lived to a painless or vigorous old age.

Many settlers had driven cattle, sheep, hogs, and horses over the Wilderness Trail. No frontier family except the poorest was without at least a cow, which was regarded as a necessity. It gave dairy products, always a welcome variant of the monotonous diet, but also it served as a far better danger alarm for Indian raids than even the family dog. It was soon noticed that most of the raids occurred about milking time, and the stampede of cattle was a more certain warning than the barking of a dog.

In every cabin the spinning wheel and a pair of wool cards were symbols of domestic thrift. The women spun, wove, and knitted the buffalo and sheep's wool, brittle nettles, and flax into coarse jeans, linsey-woolsey, and linens, and then made these into family clothing. In the winter the favorite cloths were woolens, in the summer, flaxens. When feminine settlers were not busy at this task, they had plenty of others. They made soap, candles, sugar, and beeswax.

Sugar was made from maple syrup. Sorghum was the principal means of sweetening food, and to the frontiersman it was known as "long sweetening."

The men had many duties, also. Besides hunting and clearing land and planting crops, they butchered, dressed, and cured the meat, made salt, gunpowder, and shot, and molded bullets. Few emigrants brought furniture over the Wilderness Road, because it could not be transported on horse-back.For a long while, it was impossible to import any from the east, except for the few pieces which found their way into Kentucky on "family boats." Almost every article that went into a frontier home was made by its inhabitants. As a rule, the head of the household made these in the winter, when he could not spend all of his time outdoors. There were plenty of native woods—cherry, maple, and walnut—suitable for furniture. The results were often crude, for there were few lathes or other tools, and much of the furniture and other necessities was made with an axe or a hunting knife.

Recreation and relaxation were not common. These people were inclined to be religious, but there were few sermons, and these could be enjoyed only at long intervals, and after making extended journeys. Few books came over the Wilderness Trail, and there was little opportunity for exchange of opinions. But settlers came and endured and prospered, and in time life became easier. This would have been true, no doubt, for the Lincolns, had not tragedy intervened. The life of the pioneer, Abraham Lincoln, came to a disastrous close. He had settled in Jefferson County and cleared a small farm in the forest. One morning in the year 1786, he took his three sons, Mordecai, Josiah, and Thomas, to the edge of the clearing, and they began the day's work. Suddenly a shot rang out, and Abraham fell dead. The oldest son, Mordecai, ran to the house, Josiah went to the station for help, and Thomas, then ten, was left with the corpse of his father. Mordecai, from the cabin saw an Indian about to capture his young brother, and seizing a rifle, shot the red man, and then fired on others who were now showing themselves. Assistance arrived from the fort, and the Indians fled. The experience made an impression on Mordecai that he never forgot, and it was said that thereafter he killed every Indian who approached him, without stopping to ascertain whether or not he was friendly.

Abraham was dead, the Virginia relatives were many hundreds of miles away, and Bersheba was a widow with five children. She was not the only woman in Kentucky who had been widowed by the Indians. One of the most vivid pictures of the personal dangers existing in Kentucky at that time has been drawn by Captain Nathaniel Hart, who went in January, 1783, with his mother to Logan's Station to prove his father's will. There were twenty armed men in the party. At the court at Logan's Station twenty-three widows came to obtain letters of administration on the estates of their husbands, all of whom had been killed during the past year. There were many other women in the territory who had been widowed in the same manner, but whose husbands had not left estates requiring administration.

According to the English law of inheritance still followed in this country, Mordecai, as the eldest son, was the heir to his father's estate. An inventory of this estate, found near the end of the nineteenth century at Bardstown, Kentucky, shows that, for a pioneer settler, Abraham had a large amount of stock, farming implements, and tools. His home was also better furnished than that of the average settler. Bersheba took her family and moved to a more thickly settled neighborhood in Washington County, and there her children grew up, all of them respected citizens. To one of them, Thomas, was to come fame through an illustrious son, another Abraham.

3

Who Was

Nancy

Hanks?

Among those pioneers going into Kentucky at about the same time as the Lincolns was the Hanks family, from which Nancy Hanks, the mother of President Lincoln, was presumably descended. The Hanks were also from England: in colonial records the name is spelled in various ways, as Hawks or Hankes. Between 1780 and 1790, when Nancy Hanks was born, (the year 1784 being generally accepted), there were at least six Hanks colonies in the territory then known as Virginia. In 1750 a Joseph and an Abraham Hanks lived on adjacent farms in Amelia County. Some of these Amelia County Hankses migrated to Bedford County by 1780. In an area of Bedford County which later became Campbell County lived a family of Hankses which may have been direct ancestors of Nancy Hanks Lincoln. Near by lived families named Mitchell, Shipley, and Berry—all names of families with whom Nancy Hanks was intimately associated in Kentucky.

The claim has been made that this future mother of a president was born in a log cabin near what is now Mikes Run, Mineral County, West Virginia. In 1929 a commission designated the site of her birthplace here, and six years later it was marked with a monument. It has also been claimed that she was born near Keyser, West Virginia, and a tablet commemorating that event was dedicated on May 6, 1933. In 1932 the statement was made that Nancy Hanks was born at a place now called Bare Bones on the Namozine Road between Jenning's Ordinary and Fergusonville, a site named for Barebone Creek, a secondary branch of the Nottoway River. The birthplace site has also been said to be near Leesburg in Louden County, Virginia, where, in the early years of the eighteenth century, a Hanks family and a Shipley family were members of the same church. Nancy Hanks' actual birthplace, as well as other important facts concerning her life—including her birthday—has never been, and may never be, determined.

It seems almost incredible that so few accurate accounts —records or other documentary proof—can be found concerning the mother of one of the most famous presidents of the United States. There are at present two schools of thought concerning her ancestry, both of which admit that too little support can be brought to their contentions by existing documents. The best explanation of how such a state of affairs can have developed is the status commonly assigned women on the American frontier. A woman was seldom regarded as the equal of a man, although she may have excelled him in actual achievement, and although without her presence the frontier would have been longer in coming to an end. When one traces the lineage of a family, it is the maternal ancestry which most often shows gaps or uncertainties. Who was Bersheba Lincoln? Who was she when Abraham came wooing her? Was she his first wife, or had he, as did so many pioneers, buried one wife, and did he take her as a mother for children already in his home? No one knows, and perhaps no one will ever know. It was not often that a woman's name needed to go down in writing. In settled communities, family tradition, or that of the neighborhood, often carried certain important facts from one generation to another; but when settlers moved to the frontier, ancestry became secondary. It must be remembered that, like the Lincolns, these Hanks families were migrants. They had come to Virginia from Maryland or Pennsylvania. From Virginia they had moved west.

On the frontier, strangers did not care to know who one's grandfather or grandmother had been, and did not bother those they met with a recital of their own family history. Life was in the present, not in the past, and even more did it seem to lie in the future, in the days when the land would be cleared and the red men quiet, when tall corn would lift its tassels to the Kentucky sky.

Nancy Hanks was a child of the frontier. That is all of which anyone can be really certain. She was a child of Virginia, for all who have written of her agree she was born before the Hankses started west over the Wilderness Trail. Upon one other fact her historians have, in general, agreed —her mother was named Lucy. But was this Lucy maiden or widow—a Hanks by birth, or one by marriage?

Caroline Hanks Hitchcock asserted that Nancy was one of the daughters—the youngest child—of Joseph Hanks, rather than his granddaughter, as historians in general believe her to be. Joseph Hanks was the head of the Hanks family which came to Kentucky at about the same time as the Lincolns, and he did have a daughter named Nancy. One of the confusing angles to the whole problem of Nancy Hanks Lincoln's true identity is the prevalence of the name "Nancy"—a favorite in the family. There was a Nancy Lincoln—Thomas's sister—and at least two Nancy Hanks, and cousins with other surnames who were also called Nancy. Mrs. Hitchcock states that Nancy Hanks Lincoln was born February 5, 1784, the daughter of Joseph Hanks, and was named for her mother.

The Nancy Hanks whom she believed to have been Abraham Lincoln's mother was in reality his great-aunt, and an aunt of Nancy Hanks Lincoln. This Nancy Hanks was the sister of Nancy's father, according to the best evidence which has been found. Dennis Hanks, according to his own testimony, was the illegitimate child of the Nancy Hanks whom Mrs. Hitchcock asserted to be the mother of President Lincoln. Her statements were based on the will of Joseph Hanks, which she found at Bardstown, Kentucky, and in which he named his daughter, Nancy, as well as his other children. She mentions Dennis as the son of Charles Friend and Nancy Sparrow, and states that he was "often mentioned as one of the Hanks family." There appears to be ample evidence that Dennis was the son of Charles Friend and Nancy Hanks, Joseph's daughter, who later married Levi Hall. Dennis was reared by Elizabeth Hanks, who married Thomas Sparrow. Lucy Hanks, the mother of Nancy Hanks Lincoln, later married Henry Sparrow, the brother of Thomas.

According to the best authority available for many years, Nancy Hanks was the natural child of Lucy Hanks, who was yet unmarried when she brought her young daughter over the Wilderness Trail into Kentucky. This tradition traces back to a conversation in the year 1850 between President Lincoln and William H. Herndon. The two men, according to Herndon, were driving in Lincoln's one-horse buggy to the court in Menard County, Illinois, to try a suit which was likely to touch upon the subject of hereditary traits. During the ride Lincoln spoke of his mother, and enumerated the qualities which he thought he had inherited from her. He said that she was the daughter of Lucy Hanks and "a well-bred but obscure Virginia farmer or planter." The description could have applied very well to the son of Joseph Hanks whom many believe was the husband of Lucy and the father of Nancy. Abraham Lincoln knew little about his ancestors, and had little success in tracing his family tree during his lifetime.

If it were possible to prove who Lucy Hanks really was, there would be no confusion regarding the correct status of Nancy, her daughter. Was Lucy the daughter or daughter-in-law of Joseph Hanks? The theory of Nancy's birth which made her a "base-born child" would have Lucy a daughter, yet there seems conclusive evidence that she was not, but was, instead, a daughter-in-law, and already a widow when the Hankses came west to Kentucky. It is also supposed that Lucy and her little daughter did not come with the Hankses, but with other relatives.

Much of the confusion regarding Nancy's origin appears to be due to certain statements made by Dennis Hanks, who was a cousin of Nancy's. The value of his statements can, however, be judged by certain known facts. He was but nine years older than her son, Abraham, and when Herndon questioned him about her, Nancy had been dead for almost forty years. Dennis saw Nancy Hanks both in Kentucky and in Indiana, but after her marriage in the former state, he lived eight miles away. In Indiana, he arrived a few months before she died, but lived with his foster parents, Thomas and Elizabeth Sparrow. His remarks are contradictory, and it is doubtful if he really knew much about her. He termed Lucy a sister of his mother's—of, that is, Nancy Hanks', daughter of the pioneer, Joseph Hanks. Dennis made no attempt to hide the fact that he was the illegitimate child of Nancy, but he denied vigorously that his cousin Nancy Hanks Lincoln was also illegitimate, although his statements led to this conclusion.

Herndon also based his assertions regarding Nancy's illegitimacy upon information derived from John Hanks, a cousin of Dennis's (and of Nancy's) and the son of William Hanks, who was another of Joseph's children. John's testimony seems even more invalid than that of Dennis. He was only four years old when she married, and lived twenty miles away. The year of her marriage, his parents moved thirty-five miles from Elizabethtown; and it is very doubtful if he ever saw her. Information offered by either John or Dennis seems particularly worthless when it is known they both insisted Nancy was not a Hanks at all, but a Sparrow. But this could not be, since it is generally accepted that Lucy gave birth to Nancy in 1784, but did not marry Henry Sparrow until April, 1791.

Dennis was apparently confused in his own mind. The question of Nancy's birth was no doubt raised too late for him to produce any real evidence. He could not explain why Nancy was known as a Hanks when she was, he believed, a Sparrow. He said Lucy was a sister of the other three Hanks girls, yet the will of Joseph Hanks makes no mention of her, although he names each of his children. The true explanation seems to be that Lucy was a sister-in-law, but that she was close to her relatives by marriage, and was held in deep affection by them. If Lucy was a daughter, there seems only one explanation for the omission of her name from Joseph's will. That is that she had so deeply displeased her father as to have been completely left out of his will. But there is no tradition to this effect, and he makes no statements which might lead to such a conclusion.

Lucy was not a model of perfection, whether or not she gave illegitimate birth to Nancy. This is a matter of record, for before her marriage to Henry Sparrow, she was the object of public rebuke. A Mercer County grand jury brought an indictment against her for fornication, but she was never brought to trial, probably because her marriage to Henry removed the cause of the complaint. It may have been that she was living with him as his common law wife, which was not an unusual occurence in the wilderness. She made him a good wife, however, raising a family of nine children, two of whom became ministers. After her marriage, there were no more complaints against her character.

The tradition has long existed and has been generally accepted that Nancy was cared for in early childhood by her grandmother, and that, after Lucy's marriage to Henry Sparrow, she went to live with an aunt and uncle, Elizabeth and Thomas Sparrow. But Thomas Sparrow and Elizabeth Hanks were not married until October 17, 1796, five years after Henry and Lucy were married. Nancy was then twelve—if the year given as that of her birth is accepted—and so could not have gone to live with these relatives at a very early age. Evidence has been presented in recent years showing that Nancy Hanks was reared in the home of Richard and Rachel Berry, an uncle and aunt, Rachel being a sister of Lucy Hanks, both of whom were Shipleys. This fact lends credence to the theory that Lucy was a widow, and was legally married when Nancy was born. Lucy Shipley is believed to have been the widow of James Hanks, another son of the pioneer, Joseph Hanks.

In a magazine article some years ago the story of Nancy Hanks was told with a good deal of romantic imagination. It began with the light-hearted Lucy, sixteen when the Revolutionary War came to an end, and young French, English, and American soldiers, who, with the help of the feminine sex, inaugurated a post-war era of relaxation. It showed Joseph Hanks, supposedly the father of Lucy, "a small farmer, a land-owner, a member of the Established Church," and, through marriage, related to the neighboring great house of Lee, worried, despondent, disapproving, because of the temptations which faced his children in this lax environment. The Hankses leave Tidewater Virginia, move westward, where life is simpler and less frivolous. On a quiet hillside in West Virginia, Joseph settles with his family, and thinks them safe, but his pretty, spirited Lucy finds a lover, and little Nancy is born. And Joseph, heavy-hearted, mortgages his farm and turns west again, hoping that on some farther frontier he can find the haven of security he wants for his children. Over the Alleghenies, along the Wilderness Road, into the hills of Kentucky, he leads his large family. Even here, life is not tranquil, for one daughter, Nancy, bears Dennis, also an illegitimate child, and Lucy, the irrepressible, is called to appear before the court on a charge no woman could answer lightly. But Nancy marries, and so does Lucy, and the charge is dropped, and, as the years pass, forgotten, and Joseph can relax his vigilance.

If the picture were wholly true, it would not be particularly surprising, for the frontier called for quick blood. It countenanced much that would now be termed, at the least, indiscreet. War did, no doubt, as it does today, bring irregularities in its train. Young men and women who traveled the wilderness trails were not always decorous, restrained, model ladies and gentlemen. Love came early on the frontier, and marriage often before a girl had left childhood wholly behind. Illegitimate children were not welcomed, but neither were they punished, and their parents

with them, as severely as they would have been in a more
settled environment. The Hankses were not "white trash,"
to permit consistent moral lapses, but if one or two did
occur, in that particular time, and in the frontier neighbor-
hoods in which they lived, these would have been less severely criticized than in a different age and setting. Dennis
was no doubt an illegitimate child, but he never seemed to
feel any injustice in the circumstances of his birth. He accepted the fact and forgot, or never fully realized, its im-
plications. Nancy, he asserted stoutly, was "deep in the
stalk of the Hankses," but a true-born child, although he
was never able satisfactorily to explain this statement.

The other theory regarding Nancy Hanks' birth makes
her the daughter of Lucy Shipley Hanks, a young widow,
the daughter-in-law of Joseph Hanks. Nancy is presumably
the daughter of James Hanks. There is a tradition that
Joseph Hanks had a son James, who died before the Hanks
family moved to Kentucky, and that his widow came on
later with her own people. Lucy was said to be a daughter
of Robert Shipley. The Hankses and Shipleys were closely
associated over a period of years both in Maryland and in
Virginia. They can be traced from one community to another, and finally Bedford County, Virginia, became the
center of these families. There has been a tradition in existence for a long while—many decades—that Nancy Hanks
was born in James Hanks' cabin on Little Falling River.
Tradition also says that Joseph Hanks of Kentucky had, in
1793, five living sons: Thomas, Joshua, William, Charles,
and Joseph, Jr. William, who married that year, named his
first son, born the following year, James and named his
next three sons for living brothers. It seems credible that
he may have named the first son for a dead brother. Also

Nancy Hanks, the wife of Thomas Lincoln, may herself have been named for an aunt, Nancy Hanks, the youngest sister of her supposed father, James Hanks. This Nancy married Levi Hall, and named one of her sons James. The family history of Thomas, Joshua, and Charles Hanks is unknown. As yet, there is no documentary proof that one James Hanks was the father of Nancy Hanks Lincoln; but neither is there any record in existence which would make her illegitimate.

There are said to have been six girls in Robert Shipley's family of children, but only five of them have been accounted for. These are Rachel, who married Richard Berry; Ann, who married David McCord; Naomi, who married Robert Mitchell; Margaret, who married Robert Sloan; and Lucy, who married James Hanks, and later, Henry Sparrow. Statements have been made by a number of descendants of these sisters which verify the supposition that Lucy Shipley was the mother of Nancy Hanks, a legitimate child.

As a small child, Nancy is said by some to have lived in the Catawba River country in North Carolina, coming with her mother and other relatives to Kentucky about 1786. In the spring of 1790 Lucy made preparations for her marriage to Henry Sparrow. It was necessary for her to make some affirmation as to her age and her willingness for the marriage license to be issued. No Hanks name appears on her papers, nor on those, later, of her daughter, Nancy. If she had been a Hanks by birth, with Hanks men living not far away, certainly one of them would have been required to sign the papers. But instead the signatures of Richard Berry and a brother, John Berry, appear, which makes it seem likely that Lucy was a Shipley by birth, the sister of Rachel Shipley Berry.

When Joseph Hanks made his will, in which he alleg-
edly named all of his children, but in which Lucy is not
named, she had been married to Henry Sparrow for eight
months. Before Joseph died, she and Henry had had two
children. If there had been hard feeling, such as might
conceivably exist between stern father and erring daughter, it should have, to a considerable degree, at least, have
disappeared in that length of time, with Lucy a conven-
tional matron, with husband and children. Yet the most
thorough reading of Joseph Hanks' will give no inkling
that he ever had a daughter named Lucy, and it seems unlikely that he would have felt any necessity for providing
for a daughter-in-law, who had remarried so long before,
and was being adequately cared for. His own family was
too large for him to be able to bequeath much outside its
limits. He left to each child some especially named item—
to each son, a horse; to each daughter, a heifer yearling.
It is not the will of an unrelenting father, but of one trying
to be exactly fair.

Richard Berry had come to Kentucky as early as 1780. He had entered a six hundred acre farm on Beech Fork on his prospecting trip to this western country, but whether or not he brought his wife, Rachel Shipley Berry, and his children to Kentucky at this time is not known. It is probable that he had not: it was customary for these western settlers to make the first trip without their families. When, or with whom, Nancy Hanks migrated to Kentucky is not known. The Joseph Hanks family was in this area in February, 1787, when Joseph bought land on Rolling Fork. The first positive evidence of the presence of Nancy Hanks in Kentucky is, unfortunately, the indictment of the Mercer County grand jury against her mother, Lucy, in November, 1789.

Beech Fork, a tributary of Salt River, makes a gigantic horseshoe as it wanders through the central part of Washington County, Kentucky. In doing so, it sets aside a part of the country known as Beechland. Into this territory came Bersheba Lincoln, in the late fall of 1786, with her young children, after Abraham had been massacred on his wilderness farm near Louisville. And here also lived Richard and Rachel Berry. When Lucy Hanks remarried, it is said that she sent little Nancy to live with her Uncle Richard and Aunt Rachel Berry, in Beechland, about a mile from the Lincoln home. The tradition has long existed that Nancy and Thomas Lincoln first met when the young frontiersman went to learn the carpenter's trade from a certain Joseph Hanks, an uncle of Nancy's. There is no evidence to support this tradition. After the death of his father, Joseph Hanks, Jr., had returned to Virginia;

how long he stayed there is not known. It was not until 1805 that he was listed in the Hardin County tax books, and he then owned land in Breckinridge County, and was supposed to be living there. He is not known to have lived in Elizabethtown, where he is said to have taught Thomas his trade, until after his marriage in 1810, and Thomas and Nancy had then been married for four years. It is probable that Thomas and Nancy lived as children in the same neighborhood, and grew up together.

Richard and Rachel Berry had several children. Richard, Jr., and John were married before Nancy came into the home to live, but Francis and Edward were still living there. There were two Negro slaves in the Berry home, Nan, and her daughter, Hannah, and it is unlikely that Nancy was expected to do much hard work. She was no doubt treated much as a daughter of the house would have been.

The most adventurous period in Kentucky's history lasted well into Nancy's womanhood. One of the most thrilling experiences in her life must have been her childhood journey over the Wilderness Trail, and she was old enough to have remembered it. She had been born and had lived for a few years in the Virginia, and possibly the Carolina, backwoods, and had come west over the Trail when it was only a pack road. She probably traveled like other small children, in a large basket securely fastened to her mother's saddle. When she grew too weary of riding, she would be allowed to walk. No doubt she wore a linsey-woolsey frock, and probably new moccasins made for the rougher country into which she was going. The preparations for the journey would have been extensive, and colorful enough to have made an impression on even a very young child.

There was always a long period of talking and planning before these western emigrations began. Farms had to be sold, possessions too large or heavy to carry disposed of, provisions and clothing necessary for the trip bought or made, maps studied, and pioneers who had made the journey consulted. One Abraham Hanks had traveled the Wilderness Road with Daniel Boone, and he may have given the little colony—a family almost always moved as part of a unit—needful information. The knowledge that Indians were a real menace lay like a weight of lead in the minds of the elders, but such talk was taboo. But they counted their rifles carefully, for the strength of an expedition was reckoned, not in men, but in weapons. A man without his gun was not of any great use in an attack.

Nancy must have watched the loading of the pack horses, which carried bags of meal, packages of seed for planting in that fabulously rich Kentucky soil, simple farm tools, household utensils, blankets woven on looms by the women in the party, or perhaps heirlooms made by their mothers or grandmothers, maybe a feather bed or two. On the frontier, relatives usually settled in little colonies, and when a group moved on west, some of them stayed behind and watched with grave eyes the departure of their kinsfolk. In every heart was the knowledge that this might be the last goodbye, for even if the emigrants reached Kentucky safely, the new home was far away. Probably only the children were cheerful as the expedition formed at last for the journey.

From her place in the basket tied to her mother's saddle, Nancy could have seen the men taking their places—those acting as scouts far ahead or behind, accepting their positions with knowledge of the responsibility these carried.

The men and boys marched at the head and end of the train, carrying their rifles in their hands, with powder-horn and bullet-pouch within easy reach, and with tomahawk and hunting knife stuck in their belts. The pack horses, heavily laden, moved slowly. If there were wagons, these would be sold long before the destination of these pioneers was reached, for they could not travel the Wilderness Road. The new home would be reached on foot, or on horseback, and of the possessions with which a group started, only the most essential would be retained until the end of the journey.

Beyond the first low hill, they passed out of sight of their old homes, and thoughts were focused on the long and dangerous journey. The Wilderness Road began at the Block House in Virginia, five miles northeast of the South Fork of the Holston River at the mouth of Reedy Creek, and almost a mile north of the North Carolina line. It stood at the entrance to the wilderness, and was the last station on the road to Kentucky in the Holston settlement. Here the roads from Virginia and Pennsylvania and Carolina came together, and west of it there was only one road —the trail to Kentucky. Leaving the Block House the road ran over mountains to Cumberland Gap, climbed this gap, and found another one in Pine Mountain, and threaded its way for a hundred miles through the foothills of the Cumberland Mountains in eastern Kentucky, coming out at Crab Orchard.

Nancy, although only a child, must have remembered the excitement when the party came to Cumberland Gap, and the lowered voices and muffling of the pack horses' bells when they left this entrance into the mountains. For they had now entered upon the really dangerous part of

the journey. From here on, they must move quietly, maintain the strictest guard, do without camp fires, and in every
way try to keep the Indians from knowing their exact
location. Nancy was cautioned not to shout or cry out, nor
to laugh loudly. The journey became increasingly tiring,
for the children were more and more closely confined to
their baskets, and had less opportunity to run about and
play, or to sit by the campfire at night, listening to the
tales or ballads which had enlivened the earlier stages of
the migration.

For almost the whole length, the Wilderness Road followed the streams. It crossed rivers of considerable size.
Riding in her basket, Nancy could look down into the swirl-
ing cold water as her mother's horse found his way across
the river. Sometimes a pack slipped and some article of
clothing, some food, a package of seed, or a household uten-
sil, was lost in the water. Travel was hard, but the pioneers had expected it to be so, and Nancy probably heard
little complaint.

Before they reached Crab Orchard, Nancy would have
heard talk of other emigrants who expected to join the
party for the remainder of the journey. It is possible some
had already been encountered at the Block House, and an
advertisement may have been inserted in a Virginia paper
for fellow travelers, setting a time and place of meeting.
Often emigrants waited at Crab Orchard for travelers going west, so that there would be more rifles in case of an
Indian attack.

There would have been no lack of provisions. Nancy
must have eaten journey-cake, baked on hot stones, bacon,
and wild turkeys killed on the way. There was always
game. Bear tracks were frequently seen in the mud. At

night the scream of the wildcat or the howl of the wolf broke the silence, and the men listened to be sure these were not Indian signals. As the trail ran farther west, deeper into the wilderness, the scenery took on a wilder beauty. The little party was shut in by the mountains, whose sides were covered with timber, with grapevines, wild crabapple trees, pink laurel, and showers of rhododendron. Sometimes they could hear the sound of a waterfall in the distance.

So far as is known, this group of pioneers reached Kentucky safely. Here, unless the men had made an earlier prospecting trip, they stopped at a stockade until claims could be located and cabins built, and even after they had decided where to settle, their cabins may have been within a stockade. The gate of the station to which they first came would have ben opened cautiously, and the emigrants, men, women, children, and animals, would have entered at a run, in order that any Indian lingering near might not have an opportunity to attack while the gate was open. This was bolted with great wooden bars. However small Nancy was when she came to Kentucky, she must have remembered many things about this western trip.

Kentucky was known all through the east as a land not only of promise, but of great beauty. None could equal the Kentuckians in boasting. One of these said there was no place on the "universal arth like Ol' Kaintuck; she whips all *out west* in prettiness; you might boil down creation and not get such another state out of it." It lay in the great hardwood forest region between the Alleghenies and the western prairies. Before white settlement, which ruthlessly destroyed forests everywhere, almost all of this territory which became Kentucky had woodlands unsurpassed anywhere in eastern North America. There were giant trees whose trunks measured six, eight, sometimes ten feet in diameter, yellow poplar, or the tulip tree, sycamores, oaks, chestnuts, walnuts. Perhaps Nancy saw, or heard tales of, hollow sycamores so large that whole families camped in them until they could build cabins. From early summer until the late frosts, she could find strawberries growing wild, and in the autumn she could eat her fill of the wild grape, persimmon, papaw. When her chores were done, she could hunt for chestnuts, beechnuts, hazelnuts, walnuts, hickorynuts. It was a child's paradise, as well as one for hunters.

After Nancy went to live in the Berry home, she had the companionship of another girl, a cousin, Sarah Mitchell, who was an orphan. Sarah's mother, Naomi Shipley Mitchell, was a sister of Lucy Hanks'. In 1790 the Mitchells started west to Kentucky. Twenty-five miles beyond Crab Orchard, at a place called Defeated, the Mitchell party was attacked by Indians. Mrs. Mitchell was fatally wounded, and Sarah was captured and carried away north. Robert Mitchell started in pursuit of his daughter, but was drowned in the Ohio River. Sarah was returned to her relatives after the victorious campaign of Anthony Wayne in the west, and sometime in 1795 came to live with the Berrys.

In addition to the original six hundred acres on which Richard Berry settled, he had obtained a second land warrant, with which he had entered two hundred acres on Doctor's Fork, in Lincoln County, later Mercer County, not far from his home. Richard Berry probably died in 1798, since his will, made the preceding summer, was entered for probate in December, 1798. One of the appraisers of the estate was Mordecai Lincoln, Thomas Lincoln's brother. Something of the home in which Nancy Hanks had been living may be learned from this will. There were the two Negro slaves, feather beds, a table, chairs, a cupboard, two spinning wheels, kitchen ware, and the usual articles one would find in a comfortable frontier home. Each horse was mentioned by name—Blueskin, Lofty, Cherriot, a sorrel filly called Rosy. More than a dozen head of cattle were listed, a large herd for that time.

Two years later Francis Berry married and went to live on a tract of land cut off from the home place, but Edward remained at home. In 1800 Sarah Mitchell married John Thompson, and in 1804 Aunt Rachel Berry died. Where Nancy lived for the next two years is problematical, but it is supposed that she divided her time among the Berry boys, or lived in the home of one of them. One descendant of the Berry family claims that she lived with Richard Berry, Jr., whose wife was Polly Ewing Berry. In their home Nancy is said to have made herself generally useful, caring for the children, and helping with the household chores. It was this Richard Berry who signed the marriage bond when Nancy became engaged to marry Thomas Lincoln. There is also a possibility that she went to live in the Francis Berry home after the death of Rachel Berry. Francis and his wife, Elizabeth Brazelton Berry, and their three children lived in a comfortable two-story house with a kitchen annex. The Berrys were prosperous people; they seem to have looked with more favor upon slavery than did the Lincolns or Hankses. Two years before his marriage (in 1806) Edward Berry, the youngest son, listed five slaves for taxation; when Richard Berry, Jr., died sometime before the late summer of 1829, his appraisers listed nine slaves belonging to his estate. The Berrys also appear to have been people of some culture, and with considerable ability. They did not have the trouble with land titles which plagued Thomas Lincoln. The pioneer Richard Berry was probably a man in his late sixties at the time of his death: he lived long enough to give his children a substantial start in life.

5

In

Ol'

Kaintuck

The life that Nancy Hanks led as a child in Kentucky, even in the relative luxury of a Berry home, would have been a simple, half-primitive existence. The demands of the average pioneer were few —shelter, clothing, food, some association, if possible, with others. The first requirement of these emigrant families was shelter. Sometimes this was obtained in a stockade—at first it was generally found there—or in a cabin of some former settler.

It is true that the first home was sometimes a temporary shack of thatched branches, or a "half-faced camp," such as tradition has always credited Thomas and Nancy Lincoln with living in during their first year in Indiana. For this rude shelter trees were chosen which formed natural corner posts. A cabin was then built with only three sides, and with the fourth—which faced south—open. The sides and roof were covered with poles, branches, dried grass, mud, brush, anything that would shut out the wind and rain and form a protection from the "varmints" in the woods; the chinks were stuffed with dried grass or mud. A log fire was kept burning on the open side, for warmth and cooking by day, to frighten away the wild beasts and make the camp a little more comfortable by night. Sometimes a skin was flung over this opening. Beds of dry leaves, covered with blankets and bearskins, were made on the floor. These structures were only temporary shelters—if a man had any ambition at all—thrown up until log cabins could be erected. It is doubtful if the Lincolns—or the Hankses or Berrys—ever lived in such a camp, on any frontier, but sometimes pioneers had to make use of them.

Settlers were coming to Kentucky in large numbers by the time Nancy Hanks arrived. There were enough of them to help each other, in true pioneer fashion, put up houses, clear land, and do all the other necessary things. They were beginning to work together on community projects, as the old county records show—in maintaining roads, erecting churches, and even schools, appraising and settling estates.

Land had to be bought if it were to belong permanently to an individual, and many settlers merely squatted, because there was no land office in the west until 1800, and even after that a purchaser was dependent on the accident of the auction of the particular plot he wanted at the time he wanted it. But the Hankses and the Lincolns had bought their land. They were people of some means.

When land had been secured, the home was built. A space had to be cleared where the house was to be located, and trees cut for logs. Then all the neighbors came to the clearing, rolled the logs to the site of the cabin, notched them at the ends, and lifted them into place. Nails were a luxury, and were seldom used. The logs were placed alternately on each side, with the notched ends fitted together. The rafters were held in place by wooden pins, and the roof was made of bark or rude shingles held in place by saplings. When the frame was completed an opening was cut for a door, and a heavy wooden door with leather hinges was hung in this. Another opening was cut for the fireplace, usually made of sandstone, or of logs covered with clay, and the chimney was built of logs. At first there were no windows, but by 1800 small holes were cut to admit light and air, although these were usually barred to keep out wild animals and Indians. The pioneer was afraid of fresh air; night air was thought absolutely deadly. Windows were useful mostly for giving light. Enough fresh air crept in through cracks and chinks. Window glass was a luxury, and often the windows were covered with oiled paper. Paper, too, was rare in isolated cabins, and sometimes a marriage paper, or other valuable document carried west by a family, was used to cover a window.

Nancy and Thomas Lincoln lived in cabins like these, and their children were born in log houses. These were not the abodes of poor whites alone, but the usual homes of the western settlers and their children, for more than one generation.

The floor of a log cabin was often of earth, although sometimes a flooring was made of puncheons—logs which had been split through the middle and laid with the more or less flat surfaces on top. These early homes were generally situated close to a spring or clear brook, where drinking water could be found.

A frontier cabin was not a thing of beauty, but it had the artistic virtue of suiting its environment. It was seldom large, because the method of construction prohibited size, and it generally measured between fifteen and eighteen feet in length, and twelve and fourteen feet in width. Sometimes it was divided into two rooms by a partition, but usually it remained a single cabin, in which the family ate, slept, dressed and undressed, entertained guests, and worked. There could be little privacy. Often a loft was constructed, where the children slept, going up and down on a rude ladder made of boards fastened to the side of the room.

Cabin furniture was crude and usually homemade. When Thomas Lincoln grew to manhood and became a cabinet-maker, he found a steady demand for his work. Many articles he fashioned are still treasured. Most cabins had a rough table, some three-legged stools, a few crude shelves, and beds which were mere bunk-like arrangements built against the walls. If there were mattresses, these were filled with straw. Covers consisted of homemade blankets, or of bear or buffalo robes.

Since cooking was done at the fireplace, most food was boiled or fried. For frying, a three-legged pan was used which was either held over the coals or placed on them. For boiling, a pot held by a crane or hook, and swung over the flames, was used. There was seldom an oven, and a skillet with a tight cover, or a Dutch oven, was used for baking. The fireplace furnished heat and light the year round, for tallow candles were less economical than firelight. Generally a family traveling west brought with it a few household items, such as skillets, pots and pans, pewter dishes, plates, and spoons. But growing families needed more things than they could carry, and at night, by the firelight, men and boys carved industriously at wooden bowls, trenchers and noggins, and hollowed gourds to be used as containers.

A frontier family was dependent for food largely on what it could kill or raise. In these early days there was plenty of wild game, and deer meat or wild ducks or turkeys were particularly welcome additions to the menu. There were always bears—the bear figures prominently in frontier folklore, for there were so many in this Kentucky wilderness—but its meat was coarse and greasy. These southern immigrants depended largely on corn as a staple food. It was used in many ways: "johnny cake," "pone," mush and hominy were some of the commonest forms. Pigs ran wild in the woods, found their own food, and were shot like wild

animals. A favorite frontier dish was "hog and hominy."
Honey and molasses were used for sweetening, for there
was still very little sugar. Milk was not as common as it
might have been, if cattle had been cared for better, and
gravy or bear's oil often took the place of milk on mush.
Vegetables were common—corn, beans, melons, pumpkins,
peas, and squash, and very early there was also an abundance of such fruits as peaches, apples, plums, and wild
grapes. Through the summer and autumn months the settlers ate well, but in the winter they were largely dependent on such staples as flour and salt pork, for they knew
little of preserving foods, and the only way in which they
could keep fruits or vegetables was by drying them.

Almost any account of the life of Thomas Lincoln con-
tains statements accusing him of being a whiskey dealer or
distiller, and of drinking. This might have been said of almost every respectable and ambitious pioneer of his time,
but the true significance of such a state of affairs can be
understood only when it is remembered that it was a long
way to any market from the average Kentucky clearing,
and the settlers learned very early that the best way of
realizing any financial returns from their corn crops was
by converting these into liquor. This could be transported
more easily than the corn itself. Corn whiskey was one of
the commonest articles of western diet. A truly hospitable
cabin had a jug of whiskey and a gourd hanging near the
door where the weary traveler might refresh himself. Tobacco was raised very early, and chewing became almost
as common as eating.

Nancy Hanks must have worn dresses of linsey-woolsey,
a combination of linen and wool. They were no fashion
models, for this was a coarse cloth, and made heavy gar-

ments. Clothes on the frontier were more a matter of necessity than of vanity. She may have worn shoes made of leather tanned by one of her male relatives, or moccasins. The probability is that most of the time she went barefoot, like other frontier women, to save shoe leather. If she found a ribbon or a treasured shawl, or some other bit of finery stowed away among her mother's, or an aunt's, possessions, and wanted to see how it became her, she could go down to the spring and look at herself in the clear water, like other frontier lasses. Mirrors were almost unknown. None were listed among the items comprising Richard Berry, Sr.'s, estate, but there were some "ten (sic) plates," which might have been bright enough to reflect her face.

There is no evidence that Nancy ever learned how to write, in spite of the tradition that she taught her husband to do so. The only time she had occasion to sign a public paper, she made her mark. Neither is this proof she could not write, as settlers who could sign their names, often simply made their marks. Abraham, her son, in after years, said she was a "ready" reader—presumably a good reader, and read the Bible to him. It is perfectly possible that she could read and could not write. If she had not known how to do either, she would have still been as well educated as the majority of young settlers. "Reading, 'riting, and 'rithmetic" was the usual curriculum, where there was any at all, but that was in few places on the frontier. Education was given only to young children, and to these only at times when they could be spared from the work of making a home in the wilderness, which was generally for a few months in the winter, and, for the youngest ones, a short time in the summer. Even by 1800, when Nancy would probably have thought her school days over, if they ever existed, since she was then a young woman in her teens, the frontier of Kentucky had only one-room log schoolhouses, without grades, and where children used any book they could get hold of as a text—"blab" schools, where they studied out loud. This was still true in young Abraham's day; his mother lived a generation earlier.

Nancy was to die a young woman, largely because of the exigencies of pioneer life. There were many reasons why early settlers seldom lived to a ripe old age. The frontier was neither a healthful nor a safe place. Men were killed by accidents incidental to claiming the wilderness. Hunting, felling trees, killing Indians, killing game for the table, encounters with such animals as bears or "painters" all took their toll. There were many vicious animals on this frontier. Wildcats, or catamounts, were extremely annoying. These were bold creatures, which would enter a hog pen or even a cabin, and, if hungry, would attack a grown man. Sometimes they stole children from cabins or clearings. Bears were both plentiful and dangerous, and the frontiersman who took a shot at one had better be sure he aimed well, for an angry bear was a formidable enemy. The panther, or "painter," was as treacherous an animal as could be found on the frontier. Then there were 'coon and 'possums—not mean, and a very valuable source of food. Nancy must often have looked from the edge of the clearing into the thick woods and listened for the sounds of those animals her uncles killed, and told such tall tales about. She was, no doubt, warned not to go to play where a "varmint" could molest her.

Children who survived the danger of death at the hands of vicious animals, or unfriendly Indians, or of capture by the latter, were exposed to the diseases which were common on the frontier. Medical practices were crude and simple. Every family had its own supply of "simples"— herbs and drugs such as calomel, jalap, and cinchona bark, which contained quinine. The early doctors, where such were available, knew little more than a frontier mother, for usually they had learned their trade—it could scarcely be called a profession—from predecessors and through experience, and had little, or no, formal training. Pioneers learned to rely largely on their own knowledge. There is only one instance in the entire life of Nancy Hanks Lincoln when there is any evidence that she called upon a doctor to care for herself or a member of the family. This is a bill tendered for services, probably in connection with the illness of her third child, Thomas, who died as an infant.

Frontier doctors carried their supplies in their saddle bags and traveled on horseback. Usually these supplies consisted of a few simple drugs, roots, herbs, calomel, a lancet, cupping glasses, and a supply of leeches. Blood letting was common, and was done either by cupping or by the use of leeches. It was done in reckless fashion, and was thought especially good for fevers. Calomel was taken in large quantities, and many a frontier woman lost her teeth as a result of the enormous amount of calomel in her system. There were all sorts of superstitions on the frontier regarding health. There were others regarding beauty. Nancy may have often, as she grew into young womanhood, have followed the belief that the early morning dew was good for the complexion, and have slipped outside the door before sun-up to wash her face in it.

6

Sunday Comes

Over the

Mountain

As Nancy grew older, she must have become interested in the social activities of the -frontier, and in its religion. She would have taken an early part in all available forms of recreation, for children accompanied their elders everywhere, and entered into as many phases of frontier life as their ages allowed. They grew up early. Very young girls learned the figures of the dances, for they, as well as aged grandmothers, were in demand in a society where women were always too few in number. It is probable that the dances which Nancy attended were what are known as play-parties; and that the dancers moved to the rhythm of their own singing, rather than to music. She had also to learn the pattern of life in a pioneer household, and to begin very early to do her share of its strenuous and never ceasing work.

At first religion had little opportunity to manifest itself actively on the western frontier, for the pioneers were too busy establishing homes to bother much with a wrathful God. To most frontiersmen Sunday was only the seventh day. In the early years at Louisville a Virginian was scolded for not keeping his store open on Sunday, and asked why it was closed. He answered that it was the Sabbath. But Sunday hadn't come over the mountains yet, he was told. "I brought it with me," was the quiet answer.

By 1800 the spirit of the Lord was making itself manifest on the frontier in a manner that was peculiarly attractive to these southern emigrants. A wave of religious revivals began in Kentucky and poured over the west with an increasing fury. Faced with the unknown wilderness and its discomforts and dangers, the pioneer found it necessary to maintain a strong belief in the importance of the individual. Religion was a vital force in buttressing this faith. Also, while frontier families necessarily lived in isolation, they did not always do so from choice. They were anxious for contact with other families, for an opportunity to exchange news, to make and strengthen friendships, to gossip, to see the new babies which appeared annually in frontier cabins, and to discuss politics and crops. The religious gatherings, particularly the camp-meetings, gave them this opportunity. Furthermore, the frontier badly needed an outlet for its pent-up emotional strains. The religion of the camp-meeting was highly emotional, and must have stirred even very young children, if not to a love of the deity, at least to a fear and an awe.

Nancy must have seen and waited on the circuit riders who came through Kentucky. The circuit rider was a familiar and welcome figure. As a rule he was picturesque, in his straight-breasted waistcoat, high collar, plain necktie, and long hair. Barbers were scarce on the frontier, and long hair was common, for a man could cut it himself, if he had no wife to do it for him. In his saddle bags the rider carried the Bible, a hymn book, and often a copy of *Pilgrim's Progress*, for John Bunyan spoke the colorful language the frontier understood. Sometimes there were other books which the minister loaned to scattered families where there was some individual who could read them aloud.

These circuit riders were "unlarned men," as a rule, and the west preferred them so. It wanted no "Prispatarians" with their restrained sermons. In the cabin homes the circuit riders were doubly welcome. Their arrival meant a neighborhood gathering, to listen to the preaching, and to get the news. For the preacher brought more than the word of God. He knew the fashions, how to please the women, and the latest inventions, and what was being done by the government, and had little anecdotes to tell of people they knew or knew of. He took the place of the modern newspaper.

No doubt Nancy and Thomas attended many camp meetings. A contemporary of theirs professed to remember having seen them together at one meeting not long before their wedding, and said the Hanks women were great hands at revivals. The meetings were lengthy affairs, lasting from Friday until Tuesday, a long weekend. Nancy may very likely have gone to the famous meeting at Cane Ridge, Kentucky, in August, 1801, which marked the height of the Great Revival, for it is said that between 20,000 and 30,000 settlers did attend this gathering. There was never one so large again, but they continued to be very popular. Nancy was then in early adolescence, and probably was stirred like other girls on the Kentucky frontier by the emotional frenzy which had the whole area in the throes of a religious revival. No doubt she traveled many miles to more than one meeting. Whole families came to these, twenty, thirty, sometimes a hundred miles through the wilderness. They brought tents, food, clothing, cooking utensils, and even furniture, and put up their tents or constructed rude cabins. A large space was cleared, the big meeting tent erected in the middle, smaller ones outside this, and living quarters at the edge of the clearing. Often stores were hastily put up, also, to provide necessary articles. Cooking was done over large fires.

Meetings were held morning, afternoon, and evening. A

space between the platform where the ministers took turns describing the horrors of hell was strewn with loose straw, and here the repentant sinners knelt. The seats were halves of split logs arranged in parallel rows. Pine torches furnished illumination. It was always the dangers of torment these preachers spoke of, never the beauties of heaven, and the crowd of emotionally starved pioneers, seated in the flickering light of the pine torches, with the limitless wilderness crowding in on every side, listened as if hypnotized. Frontier ministers who were successful were good psychologists. They knew how to gain and hold the attention of their audiences. They attacked every pleasure these frontiersmen had—"cyards," horse racing, fighting, drinking, fiddlin', dancing—all of them, and the pioneers sang and shouted, repented and fell to the ground in the "jerks," or had trances or visions, or gave barks like dogs, or emitted the "holy laugh," and made amends for their sins. Then, when the preachers passed on, they took advantage of their scanty opportunities for recreation, and awaited the next camp meeting to repent again. For these were, after all, southern emigrants, and had the love of cards and fighting and drinking and horse racing in their blood. They left a daily consciousness of sin to the Yankees, whom they never understood, and never quite trusted.

Sometimes the whiskey sold on the outskirts of the grounds made trouble. Hangers-on, who did not come for religious reasons, provoked some of those who did into a free-for-all fight. Other undesirable results were obtained from the over-emotionalism of the meeting. Sex was not always sublimated, and sometimes young people confused human and divine love. Not all the experiences an individ-

ual had at a camp meeting were certain to be spiritual, and
guards had to be posted to keep young people from wandering from the grounds into the surrounding woods.

Nancy must have heard talk of the Shaker community
at Shakertown, settled a year before her marriage, in 1805.
The Shakers, or Shaking Quakers, had founded an almost
ideal settlement on the frontier. They developed a well-to-
do colony during the years she and Thomas were living in
their cabin homes in Kentucky. They did not believe in
marriage, but aside from this eccentricity, the frontier ad-
mired them. They had the virtues it emphasized. They
held religion as their chief interest, and it was the period
when Kentucky was most deeply interested in religion;
next to that, they emphasized work. They believed in the
"gift of many tongues," and the frontier always had many
elements of the Shaker religion in its own—a certain mysti-
cism, visions and prophecies, communion with the spirit of
the departed, power over physical disease, a confession of
sin. The sedate singing, dancing, and hand clapping of the
Shaker meeting were far more restrained than the emotional reactions of the frontier revival, but they bore a
kinship.

Nancy and Tom could have been no strangers to Catholicism. Three years after the birth of young Abraham, a
log structure was erected only a few miles from the Lincoln home, near Bardstown, Kentucky, which became the
mother house of the Sisters of Charity of Nazareth. This
became a flourishing order. The Lincolns lived for seven
years in the community where the Catholic Church first
established itself in the middle west. When young Abraham was two, a Trappist Monastery, known as Gethsemane
Abbey, was established near the Knob Creek farm. His first

school teacher was a Catholic, and is said to be buried at Gethsemane. Also, Mordecai, the brother of Thomas Lincoln, married into a prominent Catholic family. His son Abraham, eleven years older than the future president, was brought up in that faith.

While Thomas and Nancy were married by a Methodist minister, they were Baptists. The Lincolns had become united with that church in Virginia, where the Linville Creek Baptist Church was built near, if not on, their land. One acre in a corner of the tract of land settled by the pioneer, Abraham Lincoln, in Kentucky, was known as God's acre, and on this was built the Long Run Church. When Thomas and Nancy lived in Elizabethtown, they were near the Severn's Valley Baptist Church, the oldest Baptist organization west of the Alleghenies. On their first farm, they were about a mile from the South Fork Baptist Church—a Separate Baptist Church—where the first baptisms in Kentucky were said to have taken place. They affiliated, however, with another Separate Baptist Church—the Little Mount—nearer their home, which was an anti-slavery church. When the Lincolns moved to Indiana, there was no church in their community, and it was not until after Nancy's death that the Pigeon Church, of which Thomas became an active member, was built. When Nancy Hanks Lincoln died, her name was still on the register of the Little Mount Church in Kentucky.

The religious experiences of the Thomas Lincolns were similar to those of their contemporaries. While there is no evidence that any of the families with which either was associated moved to Kentucky as part of a church migration—as many did—yet religion was a vital factor in their lives.

7

Young

Tom

Lincoln

The little ten-year-old boy who had seen his father killed by an Indian bullet grew up on the Kentucky frontier. In the years before he reached his majority, he was restless. He had a right to restlessness—it was his heritage, and almost his only one. Tom Lincoln had in him generations of the blood of pioneers. When he finally made his momentous move to Indiana in 1816 it was to be the fifth migration of the direct line of the Lincoln family in America, dating back to June, 1637, when the first Lincoln arrived in the colonies. The migration westward of the Lincolns was paralleled by that of hundreds of other families, for it was typically American, repeated over and over in the building of this country.

The first Lincolns who had come to America had settled at Hingham, Massachusetts. As early as 1638 four "Thomases" had been living there, as well as a Steven and a Samuel. The Thomases had been identified by their occupations—there was a Thomas, the miller; a Thomas, the weaver; Thomas, the cooper; and Thomas, the husbandman. It was Samuel who had become the direct ancestor of young Thomas Lincoln in Kentucky. By the time Abraham Lincoln, his father, had come west to his last frontier, it becomes more difficult to ascertain certain facts about the Lincolns. As has been said, it is not definitely known whether he had one or two wives, and what the last name of Bersheba Lincoln was. The influence of the frontier was already at work in family genealogy. While the Lincolns had lived on successive frontiers, the farther west they traveled, the less important writing down family history became. They were making history those years, although they could have had no idea of the importance of that history, and of the painful and often fruitless research they were making necessary for historians.

Women were not considered of great importance on the American frontier, and their activities, and, often, their very presences, were not chronicled. Too, as families moved west sometimes the art of writing, or, at least, the habit of writing seemed to disappear for a generation or longer, during which time havoc was played with family trees.

The Lincolns had not been a settled folk. If they had been, they would probably have never come to America. They had come first to Massachusetts, from where Mordecai, born there in 1686, had done a little wandering, for he was married in New Jersey, and died in Pennsylvania. His son John, born in New Jersey in 1716, had married in Pennsylvania, and died in Virginia. Abraham, his eldest son, Thomas's father, born in Pennsylvania, had married in Virginia, and died in Kentucky, massacred by red men. And Thomas himself, born in Virginia, was married in Kentucky, and fated to die in Illinois, on a new frontier. Thomas was no "white trash"; if he was not of true aristocracy, he had in him better blood than many on the Kentucky frontier.

He had been born in the year 1776. When he was only nineteen, he was mustered in as a member of a guard for the Fourth Regiment of Militia. He was living in Washington County in Kentucky at this time, but the next year he went to Hardin County and found employment with Samuel Haycraft, working on a mill-site for three shillings a day. Thomas had only the opportunities of the average frontier boy for an education, which were practically none. His father had not been poor, but his early death and the English order of inheritance had deprived young Tom of any chance at schools or formal education along any line, if such had been available on the frontier. For seven years he worked as a laborer, before he turned to carpentry, and, finally, to farming.

He was not lazy—he did the hardest kind of manual labor, and did it consistently enough to accumulate considerable sums of money, working at low frontier wages. When he worked for Haycraft on the mill race, he did not draw his pay in the form of whiskey or other merchandise between pay-days, as some of the other workers did, but took it in cash. Perhaps he was paid in the type of currency found long after his death in the old Haycraft-Berry account book, bearing this inscription: "This Bill entitles the bearer to receive eight Spanish milled dollars or the value thereof in gold or silver according to a resolution passed by Congress at Philadelphia Sept. 26th., 1778."

He began carpentry work while he was engaged by Samuel Haycraft. He was doing rough carpentry by the time he reached his majority. He had done some roaming those early years—spending a year with his uncle Isaac in Tennessee, and some time with his mother in Washington County, Kentucky. It is possible he had also gone to Missouri to visit relatives. By 1803 he had acquired a piece of property near Elizabethtown, a 240 acre tract of land, where he lived with his mother; and where he began those odd jobs of cabinet-making, and also raised stock. He probably rented this land. At any rate, he managed it, as he is known to have sold produce from it. It is of interest to note that at the time he acquired his first farm he was not married, and, so far as is known, had no plans for marriage.

Thomas Lincoln found it possible to make money in

other ways. In the spring of 1805 he entered into a contract with Denton Geoghegan to get some logs for a mill for the latter. It was an important contract, and Lincoln apparently executed it well, but Geoghegan would not pay him, and he had to go to court to get the money. This was after his marriage to Nancy Hanks, and though the magistrate ordered Geoghegan to pay the amount due and the costs, his employer fought Lincoln for a long while over the matter, trying to get damages against him. It was not until a month after young Abe's birth in 1809 that the suit was finally officially dismissed from the courts. In every hearing Lincoln won the verdict.

In 1806 some merchants named Bleakly and Montgomery, in Elizabethtown, hired Thomas Lincoln to go to New Orleans as a hand on a flatboat. He probably also helped build the boat, for such was customary in this kind of contract. He was paid sixteen pounds for making the trip, and, from some source, at the same time received another thirteen pounds in gold. It may have been in payment for helping build the boat; it is also possible that he took produce of his own to the New Orleans market. At any rate, the trip netted him twenty-nine pounds. This was just before his marriage, and Thomas spent most of the money making preparations for the event.

Lincoln probably constructed the cabin in Elizabethtown to which he brought his bride. It is unlikely that there were any cabins for rent in the village of Elizabethtown at that time. Tradition says that he helped build other cabins in the town, engaging in both the construction and the finishing.

Thomas Lincoln owned land and raised stock, as has been said, on the first piece of property of any size he bought, the farm near Elizabethtown, but he did not become a farmer until he purchased the South Fork farm in December, 1808. There is no proof for the accusation that he was a poor farmer, or too much of a wanderer, too shiftless, or too careless, to succeed at farming. He was a pioneer, living in a pioneer environment, with the hardships, not only of a farmer's life, but also of a frontiersman's life. He was the product of his particular period in history, and, if he had personal faults, these only accentuated his almost inevitable failure. Day laborer, carpenter, farmer—he turned his hand to whatever work he could find to earn a living, and did this from childhood on. But it was never easy. A shiftless man, an ease-loving man, would have settled in some squatter's cabin, living off the wild animals, eating berries and nuts and wild fruits, accepting whatever kindnesses nature felt inclined to show him. But Thomas Lincoln was no squatter, at any time, and raised stock, and planted corn, paid his debts and built cabins, fought the injustices of old land grants, and sat in church with his brows furrowed over endless disputes about slavery, as did his neighbors, with whom he had common problems and common ambitions.

8

A

Frontier

Wedding

On June 12, 1806, at Beechland, Washington County, Kentucky, in the community where both had grown up, Thomas Lincoln and Nancy Hanks were married. Thomas was twenty-eight at the time; Nancy has been variously described as twenty-one, twenty-two, and twenty-three.

Thomas must have been regarded as somewhat of a "catch" on the frontier. He came of good stock; he had been a soldier and had fought against the Indians; he was a cabinet maker by trade, was the owner of a farm and a home in Elizabethtown. He was no yokel, but had seen something of the world. Besides the trip to New Orleans— and possibly others which have gone unrecorded—he had wandered over Kentucky and into Tennessee, and possibly into Missouri, where Daniel Boone had made his home. These facts indicate that he was a man of integrity and some ambition, and would have been considered eligible as a husband by girls far better off in a financial way than was Nancy Hanks. He must have been somewhat of a dandy, too. He carried considerable credits to his account with the Elizabethtown merchants in the years just before his marriage. In 1805 he bought a hat from an Elizabethtown merchant for which he paid $8.75, a pair of suspenders for $2.19, and other items in keeping with these purchases. From existing records which he signed it is evident he could at least write his name. An old county record in regard to a land sale which he and Nancy both signed arouses a suspicion that he was more literate than is generally supposed. While Nancy merely made her mark, Thomas signed his name, and the writing in the record and the "Thomas Lincoln" in it, are identical with the signature.

Young Lincoln is said to have been tall, around five feet, nine inches, weighing some 185 pounds. He had a round face, from which dark hazel eyes looked out from under coarse black hair. He was a slowly moving, quiet individual, who liked time to sit and think, and was, like most frontiersmen, a little independent and resentful of interference. He was not pugnacious, but was known as a good man not to rouse. He could fight if he thought it necessary, and did not shirk his own defense. He was a man a girl could depend on not to show the white feather.

No picture of any sort exists of Nancy Hanks. In later years, mental portraits of her were drawn by various individuals. It is possible these were influenced by vague memories of what she was actually like, or by descriptions they had heard. Tradition tells us, at any rate, that she was dark, with brown hair, gray eyes, strongly marked features, an accented chin and cheekbones. She is said to have been slender, of medium height, quiet, and a little melancholy.

On Monday, June 10, 1806, Thomas Lincoln went with Richard Berry, Jr., Nancy's cousin, to the court house in Springfield, Washington County, Kentucky, to sign the marriage bond, for it was necessary for a young man to go to the clerk of the county where his prospective bride lived and give a bond affirming that there was no legal cause to obstruct the contemplated wedding. Richard signed the bond as "garden" or guardian. The Reverend Jesse Head, a minister of the Methodist faith who had come to Kentucky from Maryland as early as 1797, who lived in the Beechland neighborhood, and must have known both Thomas and Nancy for many years, was in the court house that day on some business. Tom saw him and made arrangements for the wedding, which occurred two days later—on June 12, 1806. The court adjourned for the wedding day, for many who wished to attend the marriage, and were either relatives or close friends, were listed to serve on juries, or had other court business. Jesse Head, who was a magistrate as well as a minister, had business in the court himself that day. It took a holiday, however, meeting the day before and the day after Nancy's wedding.

On the frontier a wedding was a great event, one of the few which brought an entire neighborhood together. There must have been a large crowd—Hankses and Sparrows and Berrys and Mitchells enough to make a gay assembly. Tom's mother, Bersheba Lincoln, and his brothers, Mordecai and Josiah, with their wives, were probably there, also. No doubt one of the brothers acted as best man; if not, one of the Berrys could have officiated in this capacity. Sarah Mitchell is said to have been the bridesmaid—Sarah Mitchell Thompson, as she had been for six years. Tom's sisters, Mary and (Nancy) Ann were also present, with their husbands. The Lincoln children had married well—a Mudd and a Barlow, a Crume and a Brumfield—and that made many "in-laws" eligible for invitations to the wedding.

The Berry cabin where Nancy and Thomas are supposed to have been married was moved in 1911 from its original location in Beechland in Washington County to a site adjacent to the Pioneer Cemetery at Harrodsburg, Kentucky. On June 12, 1931, a century and a quarter after this famous wedding, the cabin was enshrined in a brick church designed like the old Lulbegrud Church erected in Kentucky in 1799.

The Lincoln wedding must have been much like other

frontier weddings, which were picturesque affairs. On the morning of the wedding day, it was customary for the groom and his attendants to assemble at the home of the groom's father, from where they proceeded to the bride's home. Although Thomas at this time lived in Elizabeth-town, and his mother and two married sisters were living in Hardin County, his brothers had established homes in Washington County, and it may have been from one of these that the procession started for Nancy's home in her cousin Richard's cabin.

The bride's house had to be reached by noon, the usual time for the ceremony, which was supposed to take place before dinner. The narrow trails had to be traveled in single, or at the most, double file, and were often obstructed by grape vines tied across the path, or by trees felled, such pranks having been activated by a spirit of high hilarity in the guests. If there were any non-invited neighbors, this may have been done through malice by these. One other ceremony was instigated at a very early period. This was known as a race for the bottle. When the wedding party arrived within a mile or so of the bride's house, two young men were chosen to run for the bottle. The worse the path, the more obstacles to overcome, the greater was the opportunity to show one's horsemanship and courage. The start was announced by an Indian yell, and away over logs, underbrush, hills, and valleys raced the rivals. The bottle of whiskey was always well filled for the occasion, and the first of the two young men to reach the bride's door was presented with it as a prize. He then returned in triumph to the company and distributed its contents.

The vows were said: Jesse Head, as the old record reads, "joined together in the Holy Estate of Matrimony agreeable to the rules of the M.E.C." Thomas Lincoln and Nancy Hanks. Then dinner was served. This was a substantial backwoods feast of beef, pork, fowl, and perhaps venison and bear meat roasted or boiled, with potatoes, cabbage, and other vegetables. One of the guests at Nancy's wedding stated that the menu consisted of "bear-meat; venison, wild turkey and ducks; eggs, wild and tame, maple sugar, swung on a string, to bite off for coffee or whiskey; syrup in big gourds, peach and honey; a sheep that the two families barbecued whole over coals of wood burned in a pit; and covered with green boughs to keep the juices in . ."

After dinner dancing began and lasted till the following morning. The figures of the dances were the same everywhere—the three—and—four—handed—reels, or square sets, and jigs. If there was a fiddler, there were always tireless dancers to keep him busy; if these guests danced to music, there were probably fiddlers to "spell" each other. At times the women rested, or the men took time out for drinks, but there was no lull in the fun-making. A great deal of whiskey was consumed at these frontier frolics, all with the best possible of intentions. It helped make one forget the dark woods that stretched on every side, made the blood run a little faster, drove away the fatigue of months of endless toil, gave an added impetus to the spirit of gaiety. Everyone drank, and when historians accuse Tom of doing so, this fact must be remembered. He drank far less than many of his contemporaries; he was no drunkard, but a frontiersman, living according to the code of the society in which he found himself. There were toasts to the newly wedded couple—a very proper one was "Health to the groom, not forgetting myself; and here's to the bride, thumping luck and big children."

Nancy may have blushed herself at this one: if she did not, she no doubt blushed at others which were as crude. But these guests meant no disrespect—children, many of them, and strong ones, were the best luck anyone could wish a frontier couple. It took many hands to turn the wilderness into farms, and these hands were likely to be available only where there were large families. There were few slaves and paid labor was almost unobtainable. A man wanted to work for himself, to take advantage of the great expanse of free land to make a personal fortune, not to work for wages for some other individual.

At nine or ten in the evening a deputation of young women stole away the bride and put her to bed, usually in an upstairs loft reached by a ladder. This done, a group of young men did the same for the groom, depositing him by the side of his bride. The dance went on below, but in the midst of the hilarity the newly married couple was not forgotten. From time to time food and drink—"black betty," the bottle—were taken up the ladder and the bride and groom were made to eat. Bread and beef, pork and cabbage, found their way to the bridal chamber and were consumed.

Since Tom and Nancy did not settle near the Berrys nor his relatives, but went to Elizabethtown to live, their wedding guests had no opportunity to help them build a home, as they would have done had the young couple stayed in the neighborhood where they were married. When the wedding was over, the Lincolns followed the road through the timber to their first home.

9

Life

in

Elizabethtown

Apparently Thomas Lincoln took his bride to his cabin in Elizabethtown, since two days later—on June 14—he made some purchases in a store there. Elizabethtown lay on the southern slope of Muldrow's Hill and Severn's Valley Creek, a branch of Nolin, which empties into Green River. It had been first settled in the fall and winter of 1780 when Captain Thomas Helm, Colonel Hynes, and Samuel Haycraft had come there and built three forts with block-houses about a mile from each other. At that time these were the only settlements between the Falls of the Ohio and the Green River. These crude forts were later known as stations. They were made in a very simple way. The settlers dug a trench with spades or hoes or some such implements, in which they set split timbers reaching ten or twelve feet above the level, enclosing a space sufficiently large to accomodate five, six, or more buildings, and a block-house with port-holes. One never knew when it might become necessary for the settlers to leave their cabins and band together in some kind of little frontier citadel for protection against Indians, and the block-house served this purpose.

One of the earliest settlers to come to Elizabethtown was Christopher Bush, of Dutch descent (not German, as is generally stated.) Bush reared a large family, one daughter of which—Sarah—was to become Thomas Lincoln's second wife. He was entering land in Kentucky as early as 1781, and over the years received warrants for a considerable acreage. In 1793 Colonel Hynes laid out thirty acres of land as a place to erect public buildings, and called the settlement Elizabethtown for his wife; and the following year

Christopher Bush bought three lots in the town. Thomas Lincoln was thrown often in contact with Bush and his family, and it was with one son, Isaac, that he made the trip to New Orleans in 1806. Tradition says that Thomas and Sarah Bush were sweethearts, and that she refused at this time to marry him, choosing instead one Daniel Johnston. If this is fact, and not merely tradition, she chose most unwisely. There is no evidence they were more than acquaintances, or, at the most, friends. Sarah (or Sally) Bush did marry Daniel Johnston on March 11, 1806, and until his death in the summer of 1816, found herself in most unhappy circumstances. Johnston, according to the public records, was usually without money, and even in debt. When he had the chance to become the jailer in Elizabethtown in 1814, and had to secure bondsmen, the Bush family had so little regard for him that not one came forward to sign the papers. At his death, his widow refused to take upon herself the burden of administering his estate, which no doubt consisted mostly of debts. In the spring of 1818 she bought a piece of land with a cabin on it on the outskirts of Elizabethtown for $25, and settled here with her three children. After the death of Nancy Hanks, Thomas, waiting an interval of a year and two months, and needing a mother for his two children, returned from Indiana to marry her, but first he had to pay some debts, and make arrangements for the wedding. Old Christopher Bush, who had known him for many years, and apparently approved the marriage, signed the bond.

Thomas had become identified with Elizabethtown very early. In 1797 he had worked for Samuel Haycraft on the mill race just outside the limits of the town. He lived in Elizabethtown from 1803 to 1808, and was a respected and useful citizen. In January, 1803, he was one of a number of guards chosen for a prisoner in the county jail in the town, serving for six days. In October of that year he saw his first jury service. Only free-holders could serve on juries, and Thomas had qualified by buying the Mill Creek farm, his first land, only one month earlier. In the spring of 1804 he was again doing jury service, and also petitioning for the opening of what is now a section of the Dixie Highway. For three months in the spring of 1805 he was a patroller in the northern part of the county. In 1807 he acquired a lot in Elizabethtown, and probably built a cabin on it, but whether he and Nancy lived in this particular house is unknown. The supposition that such a cabin existed is bolstered by the fact that in 1808 Thomas was listed for the taxation of two lots in Elizabethtown, paying taxes on an assessed valuation of $40, indicating that there must have been a structure on one of them.

At that time hewed log cabins were replacing round log ones, and had certain luxurious touches, such as shingled roofs fastened with poplar pegs, plank floors, and windows with glass, or at least with greased paper. If it was in such a home that the Lincolns lived in Elizabethtown, it was undoubtedly the most comfortable one they were to possess, for their other cabins were located on isolated farms, and were typical pioneer dwellings. The house in which tradition says Nancy and Thomas lived was within the town limits, since it was subject to taxation; and, as a carpenter, Thomas had probably constructed the best home he could afford. Where it was located, and even the site of his lots, is still to be determined.

At the time of his marriage, Elizabethtown was the county seat of Hardin County, and was already able to supply not only necessities, but even items which could be considered luxuries. Bleakley and Montgomery ran a store which was well stocked, and two days after his wedding, Thomas had one-half set of knives and forks for five shillings and three skeins of silk for three pence charged to his credit. There were other stores in Elizabethtown, also, but the day book of Bleakly and Montgomery for 1806 probably lists all of the things available at any of these. Already readymade articles could be purchased; subscriptions for newspapers could be placed; a wide variety of household articles, cloth, medicines, and groceries could be bought. It is not likely that Thomas and Nancy were able to afford more than necessities, but it is obvious that during their stay in Elizabethtown they were farther from the frontier than at any other period in their marriage.

On February 10, 1807 the first child of the Lincolns—a girl named Sarah, who has been mistakenly called Nancy —was born. It has been said that she was named Nancy by her parents, and later called Sarah after her father had married for the second time, after Sarah Bush Johnston. But she was named Sarah by her father and mother, and always bore this name. During the months preceding little Sarah's birth Nancy was no doubt worried by the lawsuit Tom was waging with Geoghegan, trying to collect the money due him for hewing logs for a mill. While the suit dragged on, he was doing his duty as a citizen—serving on juries, and also trying to earn a living as a carpenter. This was not easy in an area only slightly removed from the frontier period, where money was always scarce, and where men hired as little work done as possible.

In 1808 Thomas bought the second lot he owned in Elizabethtown, and also three hundred acres of land on the

South Fork of Nolin Creek, where he first attempted to earn a living as a farmer. He and Nancy moved to the farm, but he continued to be associated with Elizabethtown, doing certain services for the court, and going to the county seat on business.

Tom had to find time from farming to serve as road surveyor for the county. Certain men were appointed to help him keep the road in repair, but the real responsibility was his, and there was a penalty for failure to keep a road open. Every able-bodied pioneer had to help work the roads, unless he could obtain a court order releasing him from such a duty. The road to which Tom was assigned was a part of the Old Cumberland Road leading to the Cumberland River country, between what was known as the "Bigg" Hill and the Rolling Fork River. Tom believed in good roads, and probably undertook his responsibility gladly, since he was always a petitioner when there was any paper circulated in his community for a new road.

10

The

Birth Of

Abraham Lincoln

On December 12, 1808, Thomas Lincoln had bought three hundred acres of land on the South Fork of Nolin Creek from Isaac Bush, and had moved there with Nancy and little Sarah. This farm was in that part of Hardin County, Kentucky, which later became La Rue County. It was three miles south of Hodgen's Mill, around which the town of Hodgenville was later to develop. It is probable that there was already a cabin on the land, standing near a spring called Sinking Spring, facing west on the Old Cumberland Road, which ran between Louisville and Nashville. This cabin was the usual size of a log house in those days, some eighteen by sixteen feet.

Hodgen's Mill had been erected by Robert Hodgen in 1789 and lay a half mile below the confluence of the three branches of Nolin River. Besides operating the mill and farming, Hodgen conducted an ordinary or tavern, where many famous people passing through that western country were entertained. There were a number of mills in the neighborhood of the three Lincoln farm homes in Kentucky. Probably Thomas and Nancy never lived more than three miles from a mill while they were in this state. Mills were important, and many early settlements grew up around them, while pioneers fortunate enough to have mill sites on their land jealously guarded their rights to these. Hodgen's Mill, lying three miles from the South Fork farm, and eight from the later home on Knob Creek, was not the closest one to either of the Lincoln cabins, but Tom probably went there often with his corn.

When Nancy knew they were to live on Nolin Creek, and asked about the name, Tom may have told her the

old story he had heard when first he came to Hardin County
to live. About a mile above Hodgen's Mill, it seemed, on
the south side of the creek, there was a knoll which was a
sort of natural curiosity. It was about thirty feet above the
level of the creek and contained some two acres of ground,
with an almost level top. In early days Benjamin Lynn and
some other pioneers had camped on the knoll. In a hunting excursion, soon after the camp was established, Lynn
was lost, and when the rest of the company returned and
did not see him, one of them said, "Here is the Nole (knoll)
but No Lynn!" After that the creek which ran near the
knoll was called Nolin. Nancy had heard many such stories, for all over the country were places which had been
named because of some connection with early settlement.
It was a pretty enough name—Nolin Creek. She no doubt
hoped the farm would be pretty, too, but she was to be
disappointed.

The Sinking Spring farm, as it was called, was a dis-
couraging piece of land, with its yellow and red clay, stony
soil, thick underbrush, and land known as "barrens." Sometimes it was called the Rock Spring farm because at the
foot of one of its sloping hills the rocks curved inward, making a sort of cave or ledge beneath which people could
stand, and in the center was a never-ending flow of clear,
cool water. It was a fairy-like place, with moss over the
rocky sides, and with its greens and grays merging into
each other. Nancy, in the brief intervals when she was free
from her endless chores, could come with little Sarah and
sit in the coolness of its shade, knitting or sewing to keep
her hands busy while the child played. The spring was the
only attractive thing about the farm.

Nancy may have dreamed of the new baby that was on

its way. The Lincolns had bought this farm in the late winter of 1808, but whether they moved to it at once or not is uncertain. They were there very early in the year 1809, however, and the cabin and barren land were to have their just claim to immortal fame, for they were to become the birthplace of young Abraham Lincoln.

Nancy was probably very happy those months before her son's birth. She must have felt that they were getting along well, for they had a good deal of land and a fine little daughter. Dr. Christopher Columbus Graham, a frontier physician, who had been present at the wedding of the Lincolns, and sometimes visited in their home, found it comfortable, for there were milk and butter to make the food palatable, and a good feather bed on which he slept while the Lincolns "shook down" on the floor, following the laws of true pioneer hospitality. Thomas was a respected citizen of the community, and was shown to be so by the many ways in which he was asked to perform the duties of a citizen. They had money—enough to make substantial payments on land, and even to lend to those who were less fortunate when these were in need.

The birth of little Abraham came on a Sunday—February 12, 1809. It was a Kentucky winter's day, apparently not excessively cold, as on Monday, the next day, the county court in Hardin County met, many travelers were on the road, and there was no postponements of cases because of inclement weather. Who attended Nancy is not known, and she probably had no professional medical help, either that of a doctor or of a "granny woman." Dennis Hanks later claimed that he was the first person outside the immediate family to see the new baby, but his statements concerning the event were made more than a half century later, and were so confusing as to be unreliable.

One thing that Dennis, who had been only nine at the time, said was most certainly true: Nancy got little "nuss'n" at the time. Babies were more or less routine affairs, and in almost every cabin there was one born each year, or, at the most, every two years. Birth was so common that, although the mortality rate was very high for both mothers and infants, it was not considered particularly dangerous, nor anything to make a fuss over. Granny women took the place of doctors, and, if even these experienced midwives were unavailable, neighbors—or members of the family— did the best they could.

The Lincolns lived a little over two years on this "birthplace farm." It was part of an original land grant of 60,000 acres which had been divided and sub-divided until it had fallen into the hands of Richard Mather. The part of the grant which Mather possessed consisted of an 8000 acre tract. He had sold a 300 acre tract to David Vance, and a document in the Hardin County (Kentucky) Circuit Court records shows how it eventually came into the hands of Thomas Lincoln. From Vance the land had passed to Isaac Bush, and then had been bought by Lincoln. While here Thomas had farmed, hunted, and had done carpentry work for other settlers. He had paid cash for his land, but it was not long before he learned that he had been deceived about the prior claim of the original owner. The obligation was larger than had been represented, and the holder of the title wanted money instead of merchandise, as had been agreed. The property fell into litigation, and Lincoln lost the farm. The court ordered that Thomas should receive back the $200 he had paid Isaac Bush, but when he left Kentucky he had still not been paid the money, and had also spent a considerable sum in defending the suit. In the meantime he had bought a farm in the rich bottom land along Knob Creek, and to this he took his family in 1811.

In 1837 the court ordered the land surveyed, and the terms in which the survey was made were typical of frontier descriptions. The use of certain trees to indicate boundaries, and the destruction of these trees, was one of the reasons why pioneer settlements had so many disputes concerning land titles. The survey read:

> "Beginning at a large white oak 13 poles above the sinking or rock spring, running thence to a North 9½ degrees West 155 poles to a stake in John Taylor's field, thence South 89½ degrees East 155 poles to a forked black jack, thence South 9½ degrees East 310 poles to a black jack, thence North 89½ degrees West 155 poles to the beginning."

The "large white oak" still stands. As early at 1805 it had been marked as the beginning of the 300 acre tract which David Vance had bought from Richard Mather. It was the beginning corner of four other farm surveys, and bore the initials "D.V." Marking, or initialing, trees was another source of confusion in proving land titles.

II

The

Knob Creek

Farm

The farm homes of the Lincolns in Kentucky lay in the knob country. South of Elizabethtown the road wound between the knobs, lumpy outcroppings, some of which were denuded of everything except grass, others with small patches of timber near their crowns. In the summer the little clearings made a kind of patchwork on their sides, the light green of the tall cornstalks blending with the darker green of tiny tobacco patches, and the mottled grass and rough fields forming large irregular patches encircling them. The Sinking Spring farm had been very poor soil, but that on the new farm was rich. The knobs rose to the height of small mountains, and sloped steeply to the creekbed, towering over the cornfields and the little cabins. It was a beautiful country.

Knob Creek was a little stream flowing into the Rolling Fork River, and the new cabin was located on the slope of a hill. The farm was composed of three fields. It lay in a valley, and all about it rose high hills, and in these were cut deep gorges. When a heavy rain fell, the water would come rushing down the hills through these gorges, and spread over the little farm. Thomas sometimes got boys in the neighborhood to help plant corn in the largest of the three fields, which contained about seven acres. While they did this, little Abraham came in their wake and dropped pumpkin seed. One summer when the corn and pumpkin seed had all been planted, a big rain fell in the hills. Nancy could see it from the cabin door—a faint silver sheet far away. Not a drop fell in the valley, and she knew how lucky that was, with the seeds just in. Then she saw it coming—that minature river system of many little tributaries, rushing down the gorges, and out over the farm, washing soil, corn and pumpkin seeds before it. All the work gone for nothing, all the seed lost.

That was frontier life, farm life. But there was a strong sense of foreordination in frontier religion. The pioneer deeply believed that what would be would be, and probably Nancy only felt a passing sense of resentment against the forces of nature as she saw the seed washed away. It must all be done again—the planting—and the seed must somehow be found. Life in the cabin was a matter of routine, with daily chores and seasonal occupations, and whether these were done once, or repeated, made little difference in the monotonous round of days.

Abraham Lincoln's earliest recollections were of the Knob Creek farm. Here he lived from two to seven years of age— from May, 1811, to November, 1816. He remembered especially two things about it—a big tree and a stone house. The "great tree somewhere on Nolin River" was probably the same one Dennis Hanks inquired about after Lincoln's death: "Is the old Lunderner poplar a-standing yet?" It stood near an old mill site on one of the branches of the Nolin. The stone house would have attracted any small boy —and even his elders—and would have been remembered by all who saw it in that day of log houses. If Indians should ever decide to take the warpath again, the stone house would make an excellent blockade. The days of Indian raids seemed long past, and yet the frontier was restless until the War of 1812 definitely removed the old menace.

Soon after the Lincolns came to Knob Creek, Nancy bore her third child, a son named Thomas for his father. He was some two or three years younger than Abraham, and lived only long enough to receive a name. He was buried somewhere in the Knob Creek neighborhood, perhaps at the Little Mount Cemetery, for settlers in this area were burying their dead here as early as 1810. Some years ago a stone was unearthed in a private burying ground in the community where Thomas then lived, which bore the inscription, "T.L.", and may have marked the grave of the Lincoln's youngest child, but there is no proof that it did so.

The Lincoln cabin stood on the Louisville and Nashville road—the Old Cumberland Road. Covered wagons went by with settlers moving south and west, or north to Indiana and Ohio, and congressmen and members of the legislature passed, on their way, often, to or from the home of Henry Clay at Ashland. Christopher Columbus Graham, the doctor, who had known Thomas and Nancy now for a long time, came to the Knob Creek house. He was becoming much interested in the plant and animal life of the state, and was writing books about it. He showed them the stones, leaves, snakeskins, he had in his bag, and was carrying back to Louisville where he could study and classify them, and write down all the things he had learned. They talked about John James Audubon, whom the Lincolns had known briefly in Elizabethtown, and who showed great promise in his knowledge of birds, and might some day, they agreed, even write a book about them.

Sometimes a peddler came by, although not as often as they had when Nancy was a young girl, living with the Berrys. After 1790 these had poured down the Ohio River from Pittsburgh in search of backwoods customers. They were mostly Yankees, and were as interesting and fascinating to Kentuckians as rattlesnakes. It was believed that it was practically impossible to get the better of them in a trade, but the Kentuckians, who never shied at a horserace, or a card game, or any other form of gambling, liked to try it. They thought there was something almost morally wrong about such shrewdness in trade as these Yankees possessed, and hated them more than ever when the War of 1812 drew on, and they found out how the New Englanders really felt about it. But their women folks welcomed the peddlers, who came through the woods afoot, or on horseback, packs on back, with the universal greeting, "Hallo the house!" They were sure of a welcome, and a profit, as well.

Each peddler followed the traditional procedure. He peeled off the coverings protecting his precious goods, undid the straps with maddening care and slowness, and made ready to show his wares. But all the while his tongue was busy, cajoling the blackbrowed settler, spurring on the ready interest of the wife and daughters, telling them all the news he had gathered in many miles of tramping, watching the spark of curiosity come to life and flicker in the eyes of the father. He served as a newspaper, and knew that opposition would not endure long. The moment came when he had opened the last strap, removed the final cover. It was one of the happiest moments in the lives of many pioneer women. If they could not buy, they could always look and dream. There were gaudy cloths, calicoes, linens, silks, pins and needles, spices, hats, clocks, buttons and buckles of brass instead of the usual pewter, pans, shiny jewelry, glistening knives and razors, loudly ticking watches. Even the father lost his surliness and leaned forward to see. On the road every traveler had to answer whether or not he was a peddler. If he carried plunder, he ras a traveler; if goods, a peddler.

Now an occasional passing peddler served mostly to take Nancy back to those earlier days, when these men had been traveling stores, and a great boon to the backwoods settlements. But when villages began to develop and to grow into little towns, their usefulness was largely over. Goods were brought down the Ohio in flatboats, or over the Wilderness Road by packhorse, or, later, in wagons, for real stores, and women could make an occasional trip to such towns as Elizabethtown to buy what few articles could not be made at home. Peddlers did not care to compete with these frontier stores, and went on, to the very limit of settlement.

Nancy had help now in the house. Sarah was old enough to do many things, and as soon as little Abraham could run errands, or hold a pine-knot at night to light his father at a task, he was put to work. He filled the woodbox, cleaned the ashes from the fireplace, hoed weeds from the corn patch, and helped his mother and sister pick grapes or berries. Sometimes he went alone into the woods and came back with walnuts and hazel and hickory nuts. When autumn came, he hulled walnuts and stained his hands so black they stayed that way half the winter.

In 1816 Thomas was made road surveyor, adding new proof to his status as a dependable citizen. The Knob Creek farm was fulfilling all the dreams the Lincolns had ever had about it. It was very fertile, and a hundred years or more later would still be producing bumper crops of corn, clover, and alfalfa. Thomas grew good crops. When he migrated to Indiana, he left behind a considerable amount of corn stored in a neighbor's loft.

He made whiskey and used it in payment of his accounts, as his neighbors did. He had horses on his farm. He had always had a horse or two, and was probably interested in the breeding of good stock, for in 1815, the year before he left Kentucky, the tax lists showed he had four horses, one of them a stallion.

He spent little time hunting. Already, at that early date, civilization was driving out the wild game. It was safe for Sarah and Abraham to play outside the clearing, as it had not been for their parents when they were children. Thomas had learned, as did every pioneer boy, to set traps for animals bothering his stock, and to shoot straight and true, and no doubt had occasion to kill game, and also to go into the woods in search of it, but there is no evidence to support the traditional claim that he spent days in the wilderness, away from his home, neglecting his farm and his family. Simple as life still was, that period in frontier history had bypassed the Knob Creek area.

The children went to school a little while the Lincolns lived at Knob Creek. The schoolhouse they attended stood at the fork of what were then known as the Cumberland and Pottinger's Creek Roads. Near the site of this schoolhouse stands today a frame building—the Athertonville school—which serves the same Knob Creek community. The records of Hardin County not only locate the old school, but also show that there was a building on this spot as early as 1800. The kind of school which the Lincoln children attended may be best described by another county record—a contract between Edmund C. Tabb and eleven subscribers, drawn up in 1817, shortly after the Lincoln family had left for Indiana. Part of the record reads:

"I the Said Tabb doth agree to Teach Children Reading Writing and arrithmetic (sic) for the Sum of four dollars for each Subscribed Schollar (sic) for the Space of Six months The Teacher is to Have a Comfortable house answerable for the Business the Teacher is to

have his boarding with the Schollars further I the Said
Tabb Reserve Every Satturday (sic) in Each Week for
himself the School to commence N.B. (April 15, 1817)
and to teach good Rules and Due hours."

Abraham and Sarah's first teachers were two men, Zacha-
riah Riney and Caleb Hazel, one of whom lived on the farm
next to the Lincolns, and the other on the Pottinger's Creek
Road. Neither were itinerants, as were so many western
teachers.

Riney was a Catholic, a mature man of some forty-five
years when he taught the Knob Creek school. He lived on
a farm which he had bought from Joseph Hanks, Sr., Nancy
Lincoln's grandfather, on Rolling Fork near the mouth of
Knob Creek and Pottinger's Creek. Riney had come to this
community from Washington County, where he had known
Thomas Lincoln. He was more than schoolmaster to the
Lincolns—he was also an old friend. He had been educated
in Maryland, and was said to be a good scribe. It is possible that the Lincoln children were not under his instruc-
tion for more than two months, as in later life Abraham
Lincoln stated that in all, "his schooling did not amount to
one year." He went to five schools in the time in which he
lived in Kentucky and Indiana, and two months, in that
period, would not have been an unusually short term. There
was a court ruling that a child bound out to a guardian
should have "one year's schooling in the English language,"
consequently the Lincoln children received no more nor
less than the average frontier child.

Hazel was a typical pioneer. He was living on Knob
Creek as early as December, 1789. In 1793 he was indicted
for retailing liquor without a license, and in 1797 he was
granted a license to keep an ordinary at his home on Knob

Creek. Ordinaries were necessary on the western roads, and for the protection of emigrants, the county fixed the prices of the commodities available in them. A year later Hazel rented his ordinary. Then he bought some land in Green County, lived there for a while, and moved back to the Knob Creek community sometime before 1812. He, like Riney, was a close friend of the Lincolns. Thomas signed his marriage bond when Hazel married his second wife in 1816, shortly before the Lincolns left for Indiana. Hazel, who had been educated in Virginia, was a man of, probably, some fifty-five years when the Lincoln children went to school to him.

Only one thing worried Thomas very much while they lived at the Knob Creek farm. Sometimes he came home from Hodgen's Mill, where he had taken his corn to be ground, or from Elizabethtown, where he had gone to pay his taxes, very quiet. He would be silent a long time, but Nancy knew what troubled him. It was always the same old thing—the thing men talked about wherever they came together—the old fear that gnawed at a body's content with the rich soil and bountiful crops. Land titles—there was no peace nor relief in Kentucky from the nightmare that in some way, if a man managed to pay for and clear his acres, someone else might not turn up with a better claim to them, or so the courts would allow. It hardly seemed worth while to work so hard, with such insecurity. And while Nancy comforted and reassured him, she knew how right he was. A life of drudgery, such as the frontier demanded, such as they and their neighbors led, was a good life only if it meant plenty at the end—a farm of one's own, a home wherein safety and security might dwell, a heritage for one's children, but to work for what might be only a dream was another thing. Many Kentuckians had done so. Daniel Boone himself had lost his land and left the state, and others had been forced from their "improvements" — the cabins they had built in the wilderness. Virginia had been too busy with the Revolution when Kentucky was being settled to take thought of adequate land laws. How could a man ever be sure he had the right kind of papers?

This bothered Nancy and Thomas more than the increasing number of Negroes coming into Hardin County. They could get along with slaves and slave-owners if they had to, but nothing could save them if their papers for the land they had bought were wrong. Every time Thomas talked with other settlers who were afraid, he thought again of Indiana, across the Ohio River, which was fast approaching the time when it would be admitted into the union as a free state. That meant there would be no slavery. But, even more important, they said there was rich black land in that state, with more bushels of corn to the acre than even "ol' Kaintuck" could raise, government land with clear titles, and always the right kind of papers!

12

Black Land

and

Black Men

Before Kentucky was to come of age, it would know many troubles. In the early days there had been incessant Indian raids, and it had gained the name of "the dark and bloody ground." But its broad acres were too promising to be lost through fear of death or capture at the hands of red men. Moses Austin, coming west in 1796, described the settlers along the Wilderness Trail:

> "Ask these Pilgrims what they expect when they git to Kentuckey the Answer is Land. have you any. No, but I expect I can git it. have you any thing to pay for land, No. did you Ever see the Country. No but Every Body says its good land. can any thing be more Absurd than the Conduct of man, here is hundreds Travelling hundreds of Miles, they Know not for what Nor Whither, except its to Kentuckey, passing land almost as good and easy obtained, the Proprietors of which would gladly give on any terms, but it will not do its not Kentuckey its not the Promis.d land its not the goodly inheratence the Land of Milk and Honey . . "

When the Indians were vanquished or exiled, and capture and death had become only tales to be told around the fireside in the evening, other troubles came to the Kentucky frontier. The most serious of these were faulty land titles and slavery. Families were to lose their economic independence, to become straws on the wind, harried here and there by the ever-present land troubles of succeeding frontiers. Others who managed to keep their land were split into warring camps within individual households because of differing views concerning the holding of men in bondage.

The three Kentucky homes of Thomas and Nancy Lincoln were located within a radius of fifteen miles, and there was probably no other community in the nation where, for the first four decades of the life of this new country, such bitter controversy was waged over the question of slavery. The church was torn by the dispute, and since the Lincolns were church-goers, they no doubt often longed for a more peaceful life in a neighborhood where there was more homogeneity. They had no slaves themselves, although Nancy had lived in a slave-owning home—that of Richard Berry, Sr.—and her cousins, the younger Berrys, held slaves. Neither Thomas nor Nancy had faced the evils of the problem of slavery. They were probably decidedly anti-slavery in sentiment, since they joined an anti-slavery church, and were of the non-slave-holding class of Kentuckians.

The Lincolns had been married by a Methodist minister, but they were Baptists. This was the most active religious body on the Kentucky frontier in the early years. Thomas's father had died in 1786, and at that time there were already twenty-five Baptist preachers in the frontier field. There were also clergymen of other faiths here and there. The Lincolns must, for example, have known the famous Peter Cartwright, since he preached for a while in Washington County in 1805. He, like Jesse Head, was a Methodist.

It was with the very active Baptist church, however, that the Lincolns identified themselves. Five out of the six first Baptist preachers who came to Kentucky located in Hardin County in the same communities where the Thomas Lincolns established their various cabin homes. Two of these, Barrett and Taylor, organized the church at Elizabethtown, where Thomas and Nancy came immediately after their marriage. Joseph Hanks, the grandfather of Nancy, had bought his Kentucky land from one of these men—Joseph Barrett.

In June, 1787, Joshua Carman came to preach at the Elizabethtown church, and the slavery controversy was begun, for he was ardently anti-slavery. The next year he organized the Rolling Fork Church, not many miles from young Abraham's birthplace. Both slaves and their masters attended these frontier churches, and since slaves were not extended full privileges, Carman was probably led into an even deeper antipathy toward human bondage. He became a fanatic on the subject of slavery, and finally induced the Rolling Fork Church to withdraw from the association and to break all relationships with slave holders. In 1789 he persuaded the church to put this question to the association: "Is it lawful in the sight of God for a member of a Christian church to keep his fellow creatures in perpetual slavery?" But he was premature, and warily the answer was returned that "the association judges it improper to enter into so important a question at this time." But it had admitted that slavery had become not only an important problem, but to be treated with caution; and Carman must have felt that he had scored heavily.

Carman and the man who followed him in the pulpit at Elizabethtown—Josiah Dodge—were said to be the first preachers to separate from the Baptists on account of slavery. This community in which Nancy and Thomas lived was the stamping ground of the first Emancipation preachers in the west, and in it the question of wrong or right regarding slavery was first put to wilderness congregations. Here was organized the first Emancipation church, and here the church for the first time announced that it held no fellowship with slave holders. These ministers who opposed slavery called themselves "Friends of Humanity," while they were known in the records of the times as Emancipators.

In 1792 Dodge was preaching to four congregations— those of the Rolling Fork, North Fork or Nolin, Lick Creek, and Elizabethtown churches. Feeling had progressed beyond rebuke or caution, and when, in 1796, the question, "Is slavery oppression or not?" was put to the Elizabethtown church, the answer "was in the affirmative. It was oppression." The next month the question of fellowship with slave holders was answered to the satisfaction of Dodge—such could not exist.

The long period of unrest which characterized those early years when many non-slaveholding families were pouring into Kentucky over the Wilderness Trail came to a climax about the time that young Abraham Lincoln was born. In June, 1806, when Thomas and Nancy Lincoln first came into the community to live, a slave named Davis was excluded from the church for running away from his master. But two months later the anti-slavery members of the congregation scored when they summoned certain men to answer to the charge that they had tied up a man (presumably a slave) and whipped him. These acknowledged the report to be true, and two years later the dissension had become so vehement that fifteen members left the church because of slavery. Apparently the congregation was broken up over the question, since the records show no further meetings for two more years. The members who left the church in 1808 joined other anti-slavery advocates, and formed the Little Mount Church some three miles from the Sinking Spring farm where Abraham Lincoln was born. Nancy and Thomas affiliated with this group, although they had gone to live at some distance.

Although there were no Negroes in her home, Nancy Lincoln must often have come in contact with slaves. After she and Thomas left Elizabethtown and lived on farms, both of their cabins were on the Old Cumberland Road leading from Louisville to Nashville, Tennessee. She could sit outside the door and watch slaves raised in Kentucky being driven to the cotton markets. Often she must have likened them to cattle being herded along, for she saw these, too, pass on the highway, and there seemed little difference. There were more than a thousand slaves listed in Hardin County for taxation in 1811, an average of at least two slaves for each family. Many families, like the Lincolns, had none, but some had many. For instance, one slave holder listed fifty-eight for taxation in 1813. Some were treated kindly, as old Nan and her daughter no doubt were in the Berry home, and their services were recognized as almost invaluable, for it took many hands to maintain any standards on the frontier, and the domestic slavery of northern Kentucky was considered by many to be justified. But there were homes where slavery hung like a cloud over the family, where whippings and severe punishments and sale for profit caused preachers like the eloquent William Downs of the Little Mount Church to harangue for hours against such an institution.

A land where there was no such problem would be a sweet land. Nancy and Thomas must often have talked of such a place. There must have been one other score against slavery in Nancy's mind. This was the rapid increase in dis-

tinctions between slave holder and non-slaveholder, which
was inevitably creating social inequality. Some time later
the circuit rider, Peter Cartwright, was to say that one reason he left Kentucky was because his daughters were growing up, and he was thinking of their future. They could not
hope to marry into the wealthier slaveholding families, even
if that had been desirable. It was better for girls like his to
live in a free territory, where there was more social equality.
No doubt Nancy thought of little Sarah's future, as mothers
always have. She wanted for the child a happy, secure life,
happier and more secure, perhaps, than her own had been,
for in spite of the kindnesses of relatives, something fostered
in Nancy Hanks Lincoln a sadness.

The thing that finally drove the Lincolns from Kentucky
was not slavery, however, but land titles. Very early large
portions of Kentucky land had been obtained under Virginia
land warrants in the names of prominent Americans. Most of
these neither settled nor assigned their lands, which were
taken up in small tracts by pioneers coming into the country and looking for homes, so that certain areas came to
be claimed by several individuals. Sometimes a pioneer
would even buy his land more than once in an effort to obtain a clear title, while many, in despair of ever feeling any
security, left Kentucky for territories where land had been
government surveyed, and was free and clear of dispute.
Inadequate land regulations made trouble everywhere on
the American frontier, but probably in no other place was it
as acute as in early Kentucky.

Between the years 1803 and 1816 Thomas Lincoln owned
three farms in Kentucky. He sold the first, lost the second
because of a misunderstanding, and was ejected from the
third when the heirs of Thomas Middleton claimed the land.

This was the farm on Knob Creek, and nine other neighboring farmers who had bought parts of the Middleton tract lost their property at the same time. They decided to make the Lincoln suit a test case, and failing, in the months that followed, to get a settlement, Nancy and Thomas, with little Abraham and Sarah, left Kentucky for a land free from disputed titles and human bondage—Indiana.

13

The

Migration

to Indiana

In 1811 and 1812 a succession of earthquakes was experienced in the Mississippi Valley which made western settlers apprehensive. The first one at Louisville occurred in December, 1811. For months many houses in that town had a key suspended over the mantelpiece, with a Bible beneath the key. By the movements of the key, the inhabitants of the house could determine approximately the danger they were in whenever there was a fresh quake. Some pioneers took these earthquakes for what they were— a manifestation of nature; others thought them surely a sign of God's anger, and a call to repentance. With the superstition of the frontier, there were those who thought the quakes had some relation to the general unrest sweeping the country, which later culminated in the War of 1812. Were they signals? Perhaps, for they knew God spoke in many ways.

The Kentuckians were eager for the war. They believed that if Canada could be captured, and the United States would expand northward, the old Indian troubles that had harassed the valley so long would automatically be ended. Kentuckians had a hereditary fear and hatred of the red men, and the "War Hawks" played upon these factors to good advantage. When news came that the war had at last begun, crowds thronged the streets of Kentucky towns; and Senator John Pope of that state, who had opposed and delayed the war bill, was burned in effigy. The war was a life and death struggle in the west. In frontier cabins women were busy with the spinning wheel and the loom, in order to provide the militia with clothing.

When war came, Thomas Lincoln stayed at home. He had

a wife and two children, and land to look after. He and Nancy must often have discussed the fighting going on across the Ohio. Neighbors and friends, and, no doubt, relatives, must have been among those forces which, under Green Clay or Governor Shelby, fought bravely and successfully against the enemy. Life remained peaceful enough in the Lincoln neighborhood. Long after, Abraham, then a very small boy, when asked what he remembered of the war, answered that he could recollect only one incident. He had been fishing, and was walking home carrying a fish he had caught. He met a soldier, and gave the fish to him, "for," said Abraham, "I had been told we must always be kind to the soldiers."

It may well have been during these years, when settlers in the northwest were leaving their homes, and fleeing before the Indians, that the Lincolns gained an added interest in Indiana as a possible home. They must have heard directly from pioneers who had lived there of the rich land, and of clear titles, and the absence of slavery. For while there were Negroes in Indiana, these were either free, or the property of southerners who had taken them there from other states, and were allowed to retain their property unmolested. No man could buy or sell a black soul there, and white settlers who owned no human property felt a new sense of personal integrity.

In the spring of 1814 Nancy had something besides the war and the possibility of losing their land to think about. The "cold plague" was raging with great fatality in many sections of Kentucky. Doctors found it something new, and did not know how to combat it. The plague began with a chilly sensation, and then the patient lost all sense of warmth, and literally appeared to freeze to death. Fortunately, the epidemic ended with none of the Lincolns having had the disease.

It was with relief that the west heard, in 1815, that peace had been concluded, and the war ended. New lands across the Ohio were opened up rapidly, and the conditions of purchase were so easy that any man of ordinary industry and integrity could meet them. The Lincolns made their final decision to move to Indiana.

Nancy could not have been altogether happy about the proposed removal. It was on the women that emigration always bore the heaviest. It was they, on every frontier, who worked beyond their strength providing the necessities of life for the families, who bore children unceasingly without adequate medical advice or aid, who were required to make of their cramped quarters an ordinary for any passing stranger, who suffered greatly from homesickness, not only for friends and relatives, but for the comforts of an older civilization. Nancy had had what today seems a meager enough existence in Kentucky, but that in Indiana, new frontier as it was, was certain to be even more primitive. There were relatives already there, but homes were far apart, and there would be little time or opportunity for visiting. Too, she was leaving behind, in Kentucky soil, the grave of her third child, and it was not likely she would ever return to visit it.

The Lincolns left Kentucky sometime late in 1816, probably between the middle of November and the twentieth of December. Tradition says Thomas sold his farm for whiskey, but the truth is he was ejected from it because of a faulty title, and hence could not have sold it at all. The story told so often of the Lincoln migration north says that he made a preliminary trip to locate land, and on that trip built a raft and floated his whiskey and carpenter's tools and some household articles across the Ohio. In crossing the river the raft was upset, and everything on it went to the bottom. However, Tom managed to recover his tools and most of the whiskey, and continued his trip. He left his possessions with a settler on the Indiana side, and went inland to locate a piece of land. Returning, he brought his family across the Ohio, borrowed a wagon and horses from the settler with whom he had left his things, took them inland, and then returned his means of transportation to the owner. Then he threw up a half-faced camp, in which the family spent some miserable months, leaving it for a half-finished cabin when the Sparrows arrived. But there is no evidence for the tale. Thomas had four horses, and no doubt was able to transport his family and possessions without any help. Also, he probably only made one trip, when he and Nancy and the children went to Indiana as a group.

The story of Thomas Lincoln moving his worldly goods by flatboat to Indiana, and losing most of these in the waters of the Ohio, may have originated in confusion with an earlier incident. According to Dr. Christopher Columbus Graham, Lincoln, like other frontiersmen, had become enthusiastic about the chance of making a fortune by taking the produce of his farm downriver to New Orleans by flatboat. New Orleans was then the great market of the Mississippi Valley, and to reach it from the farms of early Kentucky was a long and dangerous journey, since first the Ohio, and then the Mississippi, had to be traversed, but if the trip could be made in safety, it did offer the farmer a considerable profit. Also, it gave him a taste of the outside world, and of a far more sophisticated one, which for many pioneers was probably a valid reason for undertaking the journey.

About 1815, close enough to the year in which the Lincolns moved to Indiana to have become identified in tradition, at least, with this migration, Thomas Lincoln built a flatboat, and loaded it with the usual cargo—deer and bear hams, buffalo, which was less plentiful than in earlier years, but could still be killed, wax, wolf and coon and mink and beaver skins, and gentian root—and floated down the Salt River into the Ohio. The neighbors, said Graham, joked Thomas for building his boat so high and narrow, and he lacked ballast for the peculiar shape of his vessel. When he started down Knob Creek it was flush with rains. So was the Ohio. In those days the floods which still ravage the Mississippi and Ohio Valleys were boons to the frontiersmen, for they permitted them to float their rafts down normally small streams.

But Thomas had trouble from the first with whirlpools and snags. He had taken his tool chest along, hoping to make some money out of his carpentry work. But the boat upset in the Ohio, and Thomas was only able to save his precious chest and part of his load because he was so near the Indiana shore. He stored these articles and came home afoot, in debt to the neighbors who had helped him undertake the venture, and his—and their—dream of quick profits gone. People, said Graham, did not make things worse by asking for their money, for in those days they "never pressed a man that lost by Indians or water," their common and vigilant enemies.

Thomas apparently knew his destination before leaving Kentucky. The widow and fatherless children of Hananiah Lincoln, an own cousin of Thomas's father, with whom the younger man had been associated years before (it is reported that he had once accompanied Hananiah to Missouri) had settled in the community in Indiana which became Spencer County, and this fact was probably directly responsible for the location of the Lincoln home on a little stream called Pigeon Creek in that state. Their home was near a famous deer lick, and was one of the last hunting grounds reluctantly surrendered by the Indians. In 1814 a traveler who had gone through this country observed that "the woods were full of deer, antelope, bears, wolves, groundhogs, hares, wildcats, squirrels, snakes, and wild turkeys," as well as many birds. Great flocks of wild or passenger pigeons were common in this region, and no doubt gave Pigeon Creek its name. There was a town some distance north of the new Lincoln home called Huntingburg, because so many people came into that section of the country to hunt the wild pigeons. Pigeon Creek was a little stream that ran into the Ohio.

Thomas no doubt took not only his horses, but also some cattle with him. If an old story of the migration is true, he drove a wagon, and Nancy and the two young children rode in this. The household stores and personal effects taken along consisted of some furniture made by Thomas, clothing which Nancy had woven and made, a featherbed, homemade "kiverlids," kitchen utensils, a loom, a spinning-wheel, and light farming equipment. In all probability, cabinetmaking, wood-working tools were safely stowed away in some corner of the wagon, and food and camping equipment were carried for the journey. The family Bible, without which no pioneer family would have felt its store of possessions complete, had been safely packed, and no doubt young Abraham had seen that his *Aesop's Fables* was not missing; while Thomas would have been especially careful to stow away the bundle of legal papers in which was written the story of his long struggle to own a Kentucky farm.

The little caravan, leaving the Knob Creek home, must have gone through Hodgenville, passing the Little Mount Cemetery, and then on to Elizabethtown, its first logical stop. The journey was slow, for the Lincolns had lived in this community for a number of years, and had friends and neighbors whom they must bid farewell.

Elizabethtown was the largest town the children had ever seen, and the only one Thomas and Nancy had lived in. It was still a village, for in 1810 the census gave it only 180 inhabitants, but it was the county seat of Hardin County. Thomas may have thought it necessary to go to the county courthouse to see if there had been any progress in clearing up his muddled land titles. From Elizabethtown the Lincolns turned north over a route once known as Bullitt's Salt Lick Trail. As they followed this road, they passed the first farm Thomas had owned in Kentucky, the one purchased in 1803.

Continuing west and north, they came to the farm where Thomas's mother and his sister, Nancy Lincoln Brumfield, were living. This was about twelve miles from Elizabethtown, and six or seven miles from the farm Thomas had once owned. Nancy Ann Lincoln had married William Brumfield in 1801, and Bersheba, her mother, had gone to live with the daughter after all of the family had married and left her. Nearly all of Lincoln's relatives and many of his friends lived near the Brumfields, in and around Mill Creek. The Lincolns stayed here several days visiting, and then traveled on west, following the old pioneer trail through Viney Grove and crossing Otter Creek. When they came to Big Spring they must have fallen in with emigrants, and have traveled with these for a distance, as this was a stopping place for parties going north, where camp was made, equipment repaired, and provisions replenished. Big Spring was located where the counties of Hardin, Meade, and Breckinridge meet. The Lincolns probably tarried here for a while, rested, and made ready for the remainder of their journey to the Ohio.

The next important point on the route was Hardinsburg. When the children grew weary, Thomas may have amused them with the story of old William Hardin, for whom the town was named, a famous hunter and Indian fighter, who had founded Hardin's Station back before 1780, and was known to the Indians as "Big Bill." They feared him because of his giant size and courage. One morning, very early, as he stood at his door preparing for a hunt, he fired his gun and began to wipe it. Just then an Indian stepped from behind the chimney and pointed his own gun at the white man. With a taunting, "Hooh, Big Bill!" the Indian aimed, but Hardin had taken advantage of the pause to knock down the other's gun, after which he brained him. In Hardinsburg, the young Lincolns had an adventure of their own. A colored woman named Minerva, the slave of a family called Murray, saw the children waiting patiently in the wagon. She brought them slices of homemade bread covered with butter, and cups of milk. When she asked them where they were going, little Abraham answered, "Indiana."

From Hardinsburg, the Lincolns traveled the Yellow Banks Road to find a place to cross the Ohio. They came to Cloverport, a river town founded in 1808. From here they continued upriver to a point opposite Troy, at the mouth of Anderson Creek, where there was a ferry in operation, and were ferried across. Then they took the road to their new home, a distance of some sixteen miles from the Ohio.

They had probably traveled seventy-five miles in Kentucky from Knob Creek to the river crossing. As early as 1816 the routes were fairly well marked, and they would have had little difficulty in making the journey, or in finding shelter along the way when they needed it. A map published in 1797 shows a trail broken from the mouth of Anderson Creek through the Pigeon Creek neighborhood, where the Lincolns were bound. They settled at a point where Lincoln City was later located, and this was the Thomas Lincoln home for fourteen years.

Thomas took a quarter-section of land in what was then Perry County, entering it in October, 1817, under the old credit system. When the government later passed a law stating that any land then in possession of a settler who had entered it might be given up at the same price for which he had originally purchased it, and the amount he was paid might be credited on any other property for which he was in debt, Lincoln gave up one-half quarter-section, and used the money he received for it to complete payment on the other one, which he retained. It is probable that at the time the Lincolns crossed the Ohio into Indiana, they were as poorly off financially as at any time in their married life. Thomas had lost a great deal of money in his Kentucky land deals, none of which he apparently ever recovered.

14

The

Indiana

Frontier

It is difficult to estimate the importance of the move of the Lincoln family to Indiana, which, while not made because of slavery, nevertheless placed young Abraham Lincoln in a free state during the years of growth to young manhood. Dates which were of great interest in his early life were also of interest in the history of Indiana. Abraham Lincoln, born in 1809, was born in the same year—and only nine days after—Indiana Territory was separated from Illinois Territory. In 1811, the year the Lincolns moved to the Knob Creek farm, the General Assembly of Indiana Territory petitioned Congress for the privilege of setting up a state government; the following year the territorial capital was moved from Vincennes to Corydon, a town in the area where Thomas Lincoln built his Indiana home. In 1814 the population of Indiana Territory had reached more than 60,000, and again the General Assembly petitioned Congress to become a state, this time with success. In December, 1816, just at the time when the Lincolns were entering the territory across the Ohio, Indiana became the nineteenth state in the union. In 1815, 318 men paid taxes in Perry County, where the Lincolns settled. Almost all of the pioneer homes were within 100 miles of the Ohio, and the area in which Thomas and his family lived was practically a Kentucky colony.

Indiana was still sparsely settled, however, and southern Indiana, where Thomas lived for fourteen years, was, in 1816, still largely wilderness. As a rule, the forests were not too difficult to penetrate, for, while the trees stood thickly, they were ramified in all directions by deer paths, buffalo roads, and Indian trails. Great poplars, beeches, sycamores, and "sugars" pushed to almost unbelievable heights, searching for air and sun, and wild grape vines locked their branches together, producing a sort of canopy beneath which animals and men moved in a semi-shade. There was little undergrowth. Here and there a storm had cut a clean strip through the heavy woods. In these cleared places bushes had a chance to grow thickly, and to give refuge to wild animals, as a few years earlier they had provided hiding places for Indians.

Life was more primitive here than it had been in the Kentucky communities where the Lincolns had lived. It was more like that which Abraham and Bersheba had known when they came to Kentucky—except for the threat of Indians—for Indiana was frontier as Kentucky had been in those earlier days. The houses were one-room cabins, usually built of round logs with the bark left on, the easiest way to use felled trees. The settlers mostly wore tanned deerhide, a material sturdy but uncomfortable when the wearer was caught in a shower. Shoes were made of this same tanned deerhide, and a wet moccasin was described as "a decent way of going barefoot." The deer was the most valuable animal found in Indiana. Deer were killed by the thousands, and provided meat for the table all through the year, while the hides were used for all articles of clothing. There were plenty of turkeys, quail, squirrels, rabbits, and raccoons and other fur bearing animals. The woods provided sweets in the form of maple sap, and the gathering at the sugar camp was especially important to the young. The sassafras shrub provided a tea, pleasant as a beverage, and important as a spring tonic. There was a wealth of berries of all kinds; the blackberry was used both as a stimulant and a medicine.

Nancy found there was little opportunity here for attending religious services; in fact, the Pigeon Church was not built until after her death. Once in a while an itinerant minister visited a community and settlers came from miles around to a meeting. If a family had a wagon, they rode in it, but as a rule the men walked and the women and children rode on horseback, the little ones in the arms of their mothers. Usually the father carried his rifle, and, if he saw game along the way, shot it. This was no violation of the Sabbath, but only sensible, for on the frontier one had to rely on the wild things in the woods for food. The meeting would be held in some settler's cabin if the weather were bad, or, if it were pleasant, in the shade of a tree in some cleared space. The worshippers brought food and put this together for a picnic after the sermon was over, or before it began. Usually they ate first, and then the preacher took off his coat and exhorted with an energy unknown in older communities.

It was quiet and rather lonely in the backwoods, even for a busy woman. Nancy must have missed the passing on the Old Cumberland Road, the visitors, the church meetings, and the various social activities that were possible when there were more settlers in an area. Here there were few gatherings in which women could take an active part. Sometimes they came together for "raisings," when a house was built in a day, or for log-rollings, when piles of fine timber were wastefully burned. The great trees, three, four, or five feet in diameter, could not be moved by one man, even with a team of horses, or of oxen. Word was sent to the neighbors for miles around that on a given day there would be a log-rolling, and, when that day arrived, the men came, with teams if they had them, on horseback, or afoot. Sometimes they brought their families, and a community picnic was held.

By using handspikes and chains drawn by both horses and oxen, the great trees were pushed, rolled, and dragged into heaps, and by nightfall the field was cleared and ready for a plough. Such fields were small; they were worked with crude implements, and only around the stumps of the trees. The most picturesque part of the log-rolling came after dark, when the logs were burned. The whole country-side would glow with the light made by a hundred great torches, and the sky would redden. Sometimes a log would topple, sending out a shower of fiery sparks. Winged creatures of the night—bats and owls—would fly above in bewildered fascination, sometimes allowing themselves to be drawn into that blazing furnace. The great fires would burn for days, and smoke would hang over the surrounding countryside, softening the atmosphere, and giving an illusion of Indian summer.

The heavy work called for equally heavy refreshments, and food and drink were provided in ample quantities. A long table would be built out of doors under the trees, and at noon, and often again at evening, the women would serve a good meal. On such occasions, the principal dish was a sort of "pot-pie," made of boiled turkeys, geese, chickens, grouse, veal, or vension, and an abundance of dumplings. There was always a supply of cornbread and milk, and a cask of rum. The men, with the superfluous energy of their generation, engaged in wrestling, the sport which belonged especially to the frontier. When supper was over and the logs blazed high, there was often a "hoe-down," a dance, with a neighborhood fiddler, often with a number serving in relays, playing away until the night was ended, or until everyone was too weary to dance any longer.

Thomas could take part in wolf hunts, when a tall pole was erected in the middle of a clearing, and a large num-

ber of hunters encircled it, sometimes forming a figure miles
in diameter, which gradually closed in with shouts and yells,
driving all the game in the woods to the pole for wholesale
killing. He could attend, which probably pleased him better, horse races, crude affairs compared with those now held
in Kentucky, more like the ones he might have seen there in
his youth. The preachers did not always agree on condem-
ning horse racing, and some of them felt the best way to win
a congregation was to engage in some of the same recreations their parishioners did, and then try to lead them to a
more austere religion. Others condemned without reserva-
tion most of the favorite social activities of the frontier.
What recreations Thomas and Nancy engaged in depended
largely upon the attitudes of their various ministers. As a
rule the Baptist churches were stern in forbidding earthly
pleasures of the sort that appealed to most pioneers. The
frontier church kept a stern eye upon members who enjoyed
unsanctioned pleasures, and Thomas himself served on com-
mittees which called upon such members. With his love for
horses, and his Kentucky background, horse racing, however, must have appealed greatly to him.

Women could take no part in wolf hunts or in horse races.
They found their greatest enjoyment in occasional weddings, entertainments as rude and boisterous as they had
been when Nancy and Thomas were married. These still
consisted of the same round of activities—the wedding pa-
rade from the groom's home to that of the bride, the race
for the whiskey bottle, a midday dinner, an afternoon of
rough games and practical jokes, a supper and dance at
night, the putting to bed of the bride, then of the groom,
and a nightlong stepping to the playing of the fiddler, with
a dispersal the next morning. Nancy may have felt too ma-

tronly now to dance. She may have sat along the side of the log wall, watching little Sarah learning the steps. Or women may have been, and probably were, so few in that Pigeon Creek community, that she stepped with the youngest and gayest of the girls. Usually even grandmothers found plenty of partners.

Nancy found here that same peculiar belief in witchcraft which she had known all her life in Kentucky—a belief which had passed away long ago in New England, but lived on in the western settlements, tinged with an African magic. Charms and incantation formed the body of veterinary practice. Luck was a powerful divinity, powerful for blessing or for bane, and to be known by simple signs. A hunter who saw a dog cross his path had as well turn home, for his luck was gone. Of course, he could, in some measure, alleviate ill fortune if he remembered instantly to hook his fingers together and pull until the animal disappeared. All sorts of signs foretold death, signs that seemed natural enough, but which had their own significance. If a dog bayed at certain hours, nothing could prevent a death. If a horse coughed in the direction of a child, one had as well prepare the shroud.

Men worked by the moon or by the sun. Plantings and sowings, the breeding of animals, and all types of farm work were determined by astronomical signs. Trees for fence-rails had to be felled before noon, and in the waxing of the moon, for if there was no moon, they would never hold together. But the moon must be dark when all vegetables which bore their fruit underground were planted, and light when those which bore their products in the air were put into the earth. These settlers had lived for generations close to nature, and they knew her great power for good or evil. They were, in addition, descendants of English and Scotch and Irish, who, across half a continent and an ocean, and two centuries or more away, had bequeathed to them, on an American frontier, folklore which still had a strong influence on their daily lives. And, in their migration to the free territory of Indiana, many of these settlers had tarried for a time in southern areas where, all unconsciously, they had absorbed much of the superstition of the Negro.

15

A

Frontier

Family

Thomas was optimistic about his new farm in Indiana. This was rich land, full of game, and with good papers which insured the fact that no one could take it from him, once he had cleared it and made it ready for corn to grow—and paid for it, which he was not to do for some little time. Nancy found two things wrong with it. The children had so far to carry water—the spring was so far away that Sarah came home puffing, while lanky Abraham usually carried the bucket alone. The other was the effect early visible on the health of the children and herself. The years of work in Kentucky, and the death of little Thomas, had robbed Nancy of much of her youthful vigor, and this new frontier would draw upon her last reserves of strength. Like other young women on the frontier, her cheeks must have long ago lost their roses, and her back much of its strength and straightness. The Indiana home lay in a marshy region, and horses and cattle sickened, and men and women came down with fever. When the children looked tired and pale, Nancy gave them Peruvian bark, but often it seemed to do little good.

Nancy was paying the penalty of her southern heritage in Thomas's choice of a farm, and was to pay it in full, as many other women did. Kentuckians—those who had migrated as the Lincolns had, down the Valley of Virginia and over The Wilderness Trail—had a fundamental distrust of the open places, and deliberately sought and built their cabins in the woods and thickets. Here they did the hardest work clearing land and grubbing stumps before they could plant crops and feed their families adequately. They exposed their wives and children to malaria and ague, and many of them died of the same diseases, but they feared the "barrens"— the open prairies—more than anything the woods could do to them. Later they followed the same practice as they turned north into Illinois and Indiana and Missouri, still seeking the timbered lands. In addition to diseases which weakened them and made them old too early, they enforced hard labor, through necessity, on even very young children. Little Abraham had an ax put into his hands as soon as he could handle one, and learned to help Thomas clear the land for corn. Children had little free time in a home like that of the Lincolns. They sowed and harvested, fed the pigs, milked the cows, fetched water and wood, gathered berries and nuts. When Abraham was not busy helping his father, he could beat the corn into meal with the flat of an ax, a chore Sally found tiring.

There were many possibilities for accidents on a frontier farm. Once Nancy thought she had lost her other son when Abraham was kicked by a horse he was caring for, and was so badly hurt that Thomas thought he had been killed. But a Kentucky-born boy had to learn to care for horses, and Abraham recovered, and did less dreaming as he worked about the farm.

Nancy must have seen much of herself in her son. As he grew older, he resembled the Hanks men, and there is a definite likeness between his portrait as a man and that of certain Hanks relatives. One day when Thomas was gone a flock of wild turkeys approached the cabin, and Abraham seized a rifle standing against the wall and fired through a crack at them. He killed one of the birds, but something made him put the rifle down, and refuse to shoot again. Thomas was disappointed. Apparently Abraham had the making of a fine hunter, and who had ever heard of a frontier lad who could not—and would not—shoot game, the very basis for life in such a community? As he looked at his son, he may have thought of the story of the frontier preacher who set his trap in full view of his crude pulpit. In the middle of his sermon, he saw that he had caught his prey, and without hesitating in his delivery, announced, "Mind the text, brethren, while I go and kill that wolf."

He felt better when Abraham gave a good account of himself in a neighborhood fight. Thomas often sent the boy to the mill with corn to be ground, as other farmers sent their sons. Abraham was like himself—good-natured, never aggressive nor antagonistic. Thomas no doubt often wondered how the boy would act when the time came to defend himself, as it must come, sooner or later, in a pioneer community where men and boys alike found an emotional outlet in rough play, wrestling, and the like, which sometimes degenerated into real fighting. Abraham went to the mill that day with no idea that he was about to be required to prove what manner of man he would become. Other lads were already there, waiting their turn, passing the time in frolicing and fighting. Young Lincoln did not take part, but stood with his back against the mill wall, watching. Suddenly he was attacked by a larger boy, with others at his heels, and Abe quickly defended himself, threshing the first, the second, the third boy, and then, placing his back against a tree, defied the whole crowd, saying he would take them all on, and taunting them with cowardice when they hesitated. Thomas forgave him the lack of readiness with a rifle when he heard this tale from a neighbor.

When winter came, the Lincolns were shut in their small cabin. This was the time of year to which Nancy's quiet, grave nature must have responded. She must have enjoyed

watching Thomas working at his rifle, or making something
for the house—the only time he had now for his carpentry
work—with little Sally knitting, the firelight on her dark
hair, and Abraham stretched on the puncheon floor scrib-
bling something on the wooden fireshovel or on a broad
splinter he had salvaged from the wood stacked outside the
door. Once he carved all evening on a knotted beech stick,
making a kind of face for the head. Abraham liked canes—
he always had one of some kind in his hand when he was
playing in the clearing, or going into the woods alone, free
for an hour from the constant round of chores. Often he
carried a dogwood club. Nancy understood why he liked
canes. It was a part of the folklore which had surrounded
his childhood, as it had her own. Witches and old women
always carried sticks—canes—and these did something to the
people who carried them. With a stick in one's hand—a certain kind of stick—one could become a changeling in this
Indiana woods, and escape, for a brief period, from the
monotonous round of frontier life.

Little Abraham was thirsty for knowledge. He had often
angered Thomas, on the Knob Creek farm, by perching be-
side his father on the fence when travelers went by on the
Old Cumberland Road, and asking questions as fast as they
could answer. Sometimes Nancy, watching from the cabin,
had seen Thomas lift a heavy hand and knock the boy from
the fence, not in a brutal manner, but as if wornout with
the boy's eternal questions, and also in rebuke, and half-
apology, for a child's impertinence. But Abraham never
meant to be rude. He wanted to know so much that the little
farms could never teach him, and Nancy wanted both him
and Sarah to have an opportunity to have that eager curiosity satisfied, to have knowledge that she and Thomas had

never had, or, consciously, perhaps, nedeed. In a community like that along Pigeon Creek, if a man could hunt and farm and talk a fair measure of religion and politics, paid his bills, and was honest and fair, he was successful. As for Sarah, a woman, thought Thomas, needed to know how to spin and knit, how to cook, wash, clean, care for sick folks, carry on a conversation without interrupting men folks, or gossiping too much, eventually how to take care of a cabin and a man and children of her own, and all these things Nancy could teach her.

But Nancy knew there was something else—something that came from the printed pages of books, and out of their words, something that she had known faintly when she read the Bible. Abraham would trace the word "Switzerland" in front of the Bible, and then the date it had been printed—"1799"—and the name of the man who had edited it, who had written a preface and notes for it, a Reverend Mr. Ostervald, and wonder where Switzerland was—if it were as far away as Virginia. Those first years in Indiana there was no school near enough for the children to attend. Abraham remembered the books he had seen once in Kentucky. A wagon had broken down before the Lincoln cabin, and Nancy had gone out to ask the wife and daughters of the man who owned it to come inside and rest until it could be repaired. The woman had brought an armful of story books from the wagon, and had read from them to Sarah and Abraham and her own children. Abraham never forgot those stories—they were the first of their kind he had ever heard. Nancy told him old tales she had learned from her mother and aunts, and sang ballads which had come long ago from England, but Abraham listened enthralled to these stories read from books, and wished he could make out the magic words himself. Sarah listened, too, and liked them, but she couldn't understand why her brother grew so excited over books. She didn't mind going to school and learned easily enough, but there was a hunger in Abraham for education.

As soon as he could write a little, he put his name on everything that charcoal would mark, and had Thomas angry with him. He liked to write, "Abraham Lincoln," and then stand back and look at it with awe, repeating the name over and over, and shaking his head. "That's me," he would say proudly to Nancy, "but," puzzled, "it don't look like me." People's names, written down, ought somehow to look like their owners. True, Abraham's name was long, and so was he. He scribbled on the puncheon floor, the walls of the cabin, the wooden fire-shovel, unrebuked by Nancy, until Thomas could stand it no longer, and got so angry with the boy that he took to marking trees his father wanted cut, or to writing his name in the sand at the deer lick. When Abraham finally secured a slate made of a piece of shale, and a pencil made of soapstone found in the bed of a stream, he felt rich. At night he lay by the fireplace, tracing a proverb over and over.

The two terms the children had gone to school in Kentucky had been a struggle, for schools were not free, and the Lincolns, like most other people on the frontier, were poor. But teachers did not have to be paid in cash, of which there was always very little, but would gladly accept corn or skins or sugar, just as merchants did.

During these early months in Indiana, the Lincolns no doubt did whatever trading was necessary at the town of Troy, not far from Hugh Thompson's ferry, on which they had crossed the Ohio. Troy was an important shipping point in those days; it is said to have been the most thriving city south of Louisville on the Indiana side of the river. At this period in the life of Nancy Lincoln, however, it is doubtful if she had much occasion to go to the stores of Troy. She was probably much less able to afford the items a store would carry than when she had gone to live in Elizabethtown, as a bride.

16

The Death

of Nancy

Hanks Lincoln

The months spent on the Indiana frontier had been hard on all the Lincolns. If, as tradition says, they lived first in a hastily constructed half-faced camp thrown up by Thomas, it could only have been a temporary structure. Within a few days, he could—and surely did —construct a log cabin similar to those they had lived in elsewhere. They may have been given shelter in the homes of relatives already in Indiana, and these may have assisted him in building a house. Abraham and Sarah were old enough to trim the branches from felled trees, cut brush, tend the fires, and, later, help clear the land for planting. Both a home and crops were immediate necessities; the time of year in which the Lincolns came to Indiana would have made the house the first consideration.

Until crops would be planted and harvested, they must live off the small animals and nuts found in the woods in such bounty, and on corn meal they may have brought with them, or which some relative could spare. They all worked hard, from the first daylight until dark, and even by firelight, making necessary articles for the house, repairing tools, preparing skins from which Nancy could make clothing. The summer passed in hard work, with little recreation.

In June, 1816, the old Pigeon Creek Church had been organized, but since this was a Regular Baptist church, or, as it was later called, a United Baptist church, with differing beliefs than the church the Lincolns had belonged to in Kentucky, they did not at once join the group. Nancy died before Thomas became a member. During the first three years of the existence of the church, meetings were held in the homes of various settlers. As the Lincolns were not members of the Pigeon Church during the early period of its organization, they probably did not even have the pleasure of listening to itinerant preachers.

Once John James Audubon, the Kentucky storekeeper and naturalist, whom they had known for a long while, came by their cabin and stopped overnight. He roamed the whole Ohio River frontier—and other frontier areas as well —looking for new birds. He knew this country well—indeed, in his book he speaks of the creek near which the Lincolns had settled. He liked to come into the neighborhood to watch the enormous flocks of passenger pigeons which had given the creek its name. He could look at the sky and see it darkened by great clouds of winged creatures, and could hear them as they flew overhead. Perhaps he knew it was a sight that naturalists who would come after him would have given much to see, in the days when the passenger pigeon would be only a memory.

He spent days in the woods, scouring fields and river banks, crossing streams, taking with him his dog, his gun, and a tin box of pencils and colors. He showed the Lincolns his drawings, and Nancy marveled at how much they resembled the birds she knew. They called him, as did their neighbors, "the bird man." Thomas thought that was a funny way to carry on business—roaming the woods and drawing pictures of birds—and wondered how he could manage a store in such a fashion, but Audubon didn't even want to talk about the store. He wanted, instead, to know if Lincoln, while hunting, or the children, while playing, had found anything in the woods he hadn't seen. The frontiersmen and their children had sharp eyes. He found visiting with them not only pleasant but profitable. The Lincolns' acquaintance with Audubon must have extended over a number of years, for while Thomas and Nancy were still living at Elizabethtown, he and Ferdinand Rozier had operated a store there briefly. Later—from 1810 to 1820—Audubon ran a general merchandise store in Henderson, Kentucky, with his brother-in-law, Thomas Bakewell, as a partner. But he was never a merchant; all his money and energy went into the wonderful project he had conceived of preserving on paper the wild feathered creatures of the frontier. He must have been a familiar figure in the Pigeon Creek area, which centered around a famous old deer lick.

Food on this frontier, like life, was monotonous. The Lincolns raised mostly corn, and used it in every imaginable way. They raised some wheat, enough, it has been said, "for a cake on Sunday mornings." They also had hogs on their farm, and killed deer, for hog and venison hams were legal tender, as were coon skins. They had a few sheep and cattle, but these were kept mostly for their contributions to family comfort, rather than as a source of profit. They provided wool for clothing, butter and milk for the table.

One morning Nancy looked out the door and saw a wagon drive into the clearing. In it were the Sparrows—Elizabeth and Thomas, and Dennis Hanks. They had come from Kentucky to locate land, and were to stay with the Lincolns until they could do so. Then Nancy and Levi Hall came to join the little settlement. Life became less lonely with so many relatives near. They all worked hard, clearing land, planting crops, watching their labor rewarded, optimistic with the optimism of the frontier, looking toward economic and physical ease with the passing years.

The crops were scarcely ready for harvesting that autumn of 1818 when an epidemic of what was known as the milksickness, or, in the dialect of the countryside, the milk-sick, swept over Pigeon Creek, killing many. The milk-sick was a mysterious disease which attacked both cattle and men, and was terrifying in its percentage of fatalities. It often terminated within three days, and settlers faced it with small hope of escape or of recovery.

Early in October the Sparrows and Halls died from the milk-sick. On the frontier a settler had to be physician, nurse, undertaker—in fact, to perform all the duties which accompanied sickness and death. Thomas, with the help of Dennis, sawed planks from logs, planed them, and made boxes to bury the dead. Little Abraham whittled pine-wood pegs, and he and Dennis held the planks while Thomas bored holes and stuck the whittled pegs through. Made by an experienced carpenter like Thomas, of planed boards, such coffins were good ones. Many frontiersmen were buried without this much attention. The bodies were carried to a cleared place in the woods and quietly let down in their graves. There was no preacher—no services.

Nancy Hanks Lincoln, standing at the edge of the little clearing as the men went about their work, could not have known how few were to be the remaining days of her own life. Probably she felt gratitude that her own household had been spared. A few days before she had visited a neighbor, an elderly woman, who said to her "Mrs. Lincoln, I am going to die . . ." But Nancy had reassured her, "You will live longer than I." Her words were a prophecy.

Nancy was sick for only a short while, and Sarah and Araham waited on her, while Thomas went about the work on the farm. She knew she could not recover, and told the children to "be good to one another," to love their kindred, and to worship God. It was all the philosophy she had ever needed, and she thought all that any individual had to have.

On a golden October day, when the leaves were drifting down to make a coverlid for her bed, they buried Nancy near the deer run. The deer, gentle, shy, creatures, were the only animals of the wilderness that frontier women did not fear. When the snow came, they ran over her grave. Abraham, watching from the cabin door—for he could not look out without seeing the spot where his mother lay— sometimes saw them running in the moonlight, and felt comforted. It was lonely in the cabin, and in the great woods, and, although he knew his mother could neither see nor hear the creatures, yet he liked to think she lay where they came, rather than in some dark and silent place in what was still a lonely land.

Index

administration, letters of, 26
Alleghenies, the, 35, 44, 61
Amelia County (Virginia), 28
American Revolution, 13, 18
Anderson Creek, 106, 107
Arthur, Gabriel, 14, 15
Ashland (Kentucky), 85
Audubon, John James, visited the Lincolns, 123; in Elizabethtown, 85, 124
Augusta County (Virginia), 18

Bakewell, Thomas, 124
Baptists, 93-96
Bardstown (Kentucky), 27, 31, 60
Bare Bones, 28
Barebone Creek, 28
Barrett, Joseph, 93
bear, tracks of, 43; dangerous, 54
Bedford County (Virginia), 28, 36
Beech Fork, 39
Beechland, location, 39, 67, 68, 69
Berks County (Pennsylvania), 19
Berry, Edward, 40; slaves of, 46
Berry, Elizabeth Brazelton, 46
Berry, Francis, 40, 46
Berry, John, 37, 40
Berry, Polly Ewing, 46
Berry, Rachel Shipley, sister of Lucy Hanks, 34; in Beechland, 39; children of, 40; death of, 46
Berry, Richard, Sr., reared Nancy Hanks, 34; signed marriage papers of Lucy Hanks, 37; arrival in Kentucky, 39; in Beechland, 39; children of, 40; obtained second land warrant, 45; death, 45-47; will, 45-46
Berry, Richard, Jr., married, 40; slaves in home, 46; signed marriage bond of Thomas Lincoln and Nancy Hanks, 68; possible marriage cabin, 70
Berrys, the, 48, 69, 85, 93
Bible, the, 57, 99, 119

Big Spring, 105; location of, 106
"Bigg" Hill, 77
Bleakly and Montgomery, merchants, 65; items available at, 76
Block House, 42, 43
block-houses, in fort, 20, 78
books, in early Kentucky, 25; carried by circuit rider, 57; of the Lincolns, 104, 119
Boone, Daniel, poor, 14; exploration of Kentucky, 15-16; cutting of Wilderness Road, 16, 41; son of Squire Boone, 19; influence on Abraham Lincoln to migrate, 20; in Missouri, 67; left Kentucky, 91
Boone, Squire, 19
Boones, the, 15, 19
Boonesborough, 17
Boone's Trace, 16
Breckinridge County (Kentucky), 40, 106
Brumfield, Nancy (Ann) Lincoln, 21, 69, 105
Brumfield, William, 69, 105
buffalo, 16, 24
Bullitt, Captain, 21
Bullitt's Salt Lick Trail, 105
Bunyan, John, 57
Bush, Christopher, in Kentucky, 73; bought lots in Elizabethtown, 74; signed marriage bond of Thomas Lincoln and Sarah Bush Johnston, 74
Bush, Isaac, trip to New Orleans with Thomas Lincoln, 74; sold land to Thomas Lincoln, 81; ordered to repay money to Thomas Lincoln, 82
Bush, Sarah, marriage to Daniel Johnston, 74; to Thomas Lincoln, 73, 74

cabin, articles in, 24; of Abraham Lincoln, 26; possible birthplace of Nancy Hanks, 28; building of

Index

Hanks family in, Nancy Hanks Lincoln in, 39; settlement of, 49; life in, 48 *passim;* religion in, 56-61; death of Abraham Lincoln in, 63; marriage of Thomas Lincoln and Nancy Hanks, 63, 67-72; life of the Thomas Lincolns in, 73 *passim;* farm homes of the Thomas Lincolns in, 83; from Knob Creek to the Ohio River, 106; land deals in, 13, 16, 20, 21, 39, 45, 49, 64, 73, 74, 76-77, 78, 81-82, 90-91, 97-98; Audubon in, 124

Kentucky River, the, 16, 17

Keyser, West Virginia, 28

Knob Creek, 60, 78, 82, 83, 85, 89-90, 97-98, 103, 105

knobs, 83

land, ceded to Transylvania Company, 16; search for, 17; on Long Run, 20; as attraction to Virginians, 22; home of Francis Berry, 46; clearing of, 49, 115; necessity for buying, 49; owned by Thomas Lincoln, 64; free, 72; on the South Fork of Nolin Creek, 76-77; how entered, 107

land grant, Sinking Spring Farm part of a, 81

land grants, 66

land titles, confusion in, 82; concern over, 90-91; in Kentucky, 92; cause of the Thomas Lincolns leaving Kentucky, 97; in Indiana, 100

land warrant, Abraham Lincoln's first in Kentucky, 20; Abraham Lincoln's second in Kentucky, 21; of Richard Berry, Sr., 45; of Christopher Bush, 73

La Rue County (Kentucky), 78

Laurel County (Kentucky), 17

Leesburg, Virginia, 28

Lick Creek Church, 95

Lincoln, Abraham, son of Mordecai Lincoln, 61

Lincoln, Abraham, son of John Lincoln, grandfather of President Lincoln, 18, 19; move to Kentucky, 20; ancestry of, 18-20; marriage and children, 20-21, 23, 29; first trip to Kentucky, 25; in Kentucky, 20-26; gives acre of land to Baptist church, 61; death of, 26, 39

Lincoln, Abraham (President), ancestry of, 18-21; confusion concerning mother of, 31; birth of, 60, 65, 80-81, 95; birthplace of, 80, 81, 94; on Knob Creek farm, 83-84; teachers of, 89-90; duties of a child, 87; left Kentucky for Indiana, 98; and War of 1812, 100; relation to history of Indiana, 108; and work, 116; resemblance to Hankses, 116; stories about, 83, 116, 117, 118; desire for learning, 118-120

Lincoln, Bersheba (Herring?), wife of Abraham Lincoln, 20; widowed, 20, 26; moved to Washington County, Kentucky, 27, 39; confusion concerning, 20, 29, 62; living with daughter Nancy, 105

Lincoln, Hananiah, 103

Lincoln, Isaac, 64

Lincoln, John, 18, 19

Lincoln, Josiah, 20, 25-26, 69

Lincoln, Mary, 21, 69

Lincoln, Mary Robinson, 19

Lincoln, Mordecai, son of Samuel Lincoln, 18, 63

Lincoln, Mordecai, son of Mordecai and Sarah (Jones) Lincoln, 19

Lincoln, Mordecai, son of Abraham Lincoln, 20, 21; experience with Indians, 26; inherits father's estate, 26; appraiser of Richard Berry, Sr., estate, 45; and Catholicism, 61